Microsoft Exchange Server 2007 Configuration

Lab Manual

WILEY

EXECUTIVE EDITOR	John Kane
EDITORIAL PROGRAM ASSISTANT	Jennifer Lartz
DIRECTOR OF MARKETING AND SALES	Mitchell Beaton
PRODUCTION MANAGER	Micheline Frederick
PRODUCTION EDITOR	Kerry Weinstein

To order books or for customer service, please call 1-800-CALL WILEY (225-5945).

ISBN   978-0-470-38030-7

Printed in the United States of America

10 9 8 7 6 5

CONTENTS

1. **Understanding DNS Resolution, SMTP, and Exchange Server 2007** 1

   Exercise 1.1: Configuring Your Lab Computers 4

   Exercise 1.2: Testing Email Server Name Resolution 5

   Exercise 1.3: Testing SMTP Support 7

   Exercise 1.4: Researching Exchange Server 2007 Features 8

   Lab Review Questions 8

2. **Working with Active Directory** 9

   Exercise 2.1: Installing a New Forest and Domain 10

   Exercise 2.2: Installing an Additional Domain Controller 13

   Exercise 2.3: Raising the Domain and Forest Functional Level 14

   Exercise 2.4: Configuring Sites and Replication 14

   Exercise 2.5: Configuring Global Catalog and UGMC 17

   Exercise 2.6: Viewing and Configuring FSMO Roles 18

   Exercise 2.7: Creating and Managing Active Directory Objects 20

   Lab Review Questions 24

   Lab Challenge 2.1: Seizing an FSMO Role 24

   Lab Challenge 2.2: Configuring a Cross Forest Trust Relationship 24

3. **Deploying Exchange Server 2007 SP1** 26

   Exercise 3.1: Deploying the First Exchange Server 28

   Exercise 3.2: Deploying the Second Exchange Server 31

   Exercise 3.3: Deploying the Third Exchange Server 33

   Lab Review Questions 35

   Lab Challenge 3.1: Performing an Unattended Exchange Server Installation 35

4. **Configuring Exchange Server 2007** 36

   Exercise 4.1: Configuring Exchange Administrative Roles 37

   Exercise 4.2: Configuring DNS A and MX Records 38

   Exercise 4.3: Configuring the Hub Role 39

   Exercise 4.4: Configuring the Edge Role 40

   Exercise 4.5: Configuring the Mailbox Role 42

   Exercise 4.6: Configuring the CAS Role 45

   Exercise 4.7: Configuring Send and Receive Connectors 47

   Exercise 4.8: Configuring an Outlook 2007 Account 49

   Exercise 4.9: Configuring an Outlook Express Account 49

   Lab Review Questions 51

Lab Challenge 4.1: Performing Exchange Server Configuration Using the Exchange Management Shell 51

5. **Configuring Recipient Objects 53**

Exercise 5.1: Configuring Mailbox Users 55

Exercise 5.2: Providing Unique Mailbox User Configuration 57

Exercise 5.3: Configuring Mailbox User Permissions 58

Exercise 5.4: Configuring Mail Users 60

Exercise 5.5: Configuring Mail Contacts 61

Exercise 5.6: Configuring Mail-Enabled Groups 62

Exercise 5.7: Configuring Resource Mailboxes 64

Exercise 5.8: Moving Mailboxes 67

Exercise 5.9: Disabling and Reconnecting a Mailbox 69

Lab Review Questions 70

Lab Challenge 5.1: Configuring Recipients Using the Exchange Management Shell 70

Lab Challenge 5.2: Creating a Linked Mailbox User 71

6. **Configuring Address Lists, Policies, and Bulk Management 72**

Exercise 6.1: Configuring Address Lists 73

Exercise 6.2: Configuring Email Address Policies 75

Exercise 6.3: Configuring Messaging Records Management 76

Exercise 6.4: Configuring Message Journaling 79

Exercise 6.5: Performing Bulk Management of Recipient Objects 81

Lab Review Questions 83

Lab Challenge 6.1: Configuring Address Lists Using the Exchange Management Shell 84

Lab Challenge 6.2: Creating a PowerShell Script 84

7. **Configuring Public Folders 85**

Exercise 7.1: Configuring a Mail-Enabled Support Public Folder 86

Exercise 7.2: Creating Project Public Folders 88

Exercise 7.3: Configuring a Public Folder Home Page 91

Exercise 7.4: Configuring Public Folder Replicas 92

Lab Review Questions 93

Lab Challenge 7.1: Configuring a Form for Public Folder Posts 93

8. **Configuring Protocols and Transport Rules 94**

Exercise 8.1: Configuring POP3 and IMAP4 95

Exercise 8.2: Configuring HTTP 97

Exercise 8.3: Configuring the Auto-discover and Availability Services for Outlook Anywhere 98

Exercise 8.4: Configuring SMTP 99

Exercise 8.5: Configuring a Transport Rule 100

Lab Review Questions 103

Lab Challenge 8.1: Configuring Additional Transport Rules 103

9. **Configuring Security 104**

Exercise 9.1: Reducing the Edge Role Attack Surface 105

Exercise 9.2: Configuring Antispam Agents 107

Exercise 9.3: Configuring Forefront Security for Exchange 110

Exercise 9.4: Configuring CA-Signed Certificates for Protocol Encryption 111

Exercise 9.5: Implementing User Certificates 115

Lab Review Questions 116

Lab Challenge 9.1: Configuring a Block List Provider 117

10. Backing Up, Restoring, and Repairing Exchange 118

Exercise 10.1: Performing a Full Backup of a Storage Group 119

Exercise 10.2: Restoring a Storage Group Backup 121

Exercise 10.3: Restoring a Deleted Item 123

Exercise 10.4: Using the Recovery Storage Group 124

Exercise 10.5: Defragmenting and Repairing Exchange Databases 126

Lab Review Questions 127

Lab Challenge 10.1: Backing Up Server Roles 128

11. Monitoring Exchange 129

Exercise 11.1: Monitoring Performance 130

Exercise 11.2: Monitoring Email Queues 135

Exercise 11.3: Tracking Messages 137

Exercise 11.4: Monitoring Client Connectivity 139

Exercise 11.5: Creating Usage Reports 140

Lab Review Questions 143

Lab Challenge 11.1: Creating Server Reports 144

12. Configuring Mobile Access and Unified Messaging 145

Exercise 12.1: Configuring ActiveSync 146

Exercise 12.2: Configuring Unified Messaging 148

Lab Review Questions 151

13. Configuring High Availability 152

Exercise 13.1: Configuring Local Continuous Replication 153

Exercise 13.2: Configuring Standby Continuous Replication 155

Lab Review Questions 157

LAB 1
UNDERSTANDING DNS RESOLUTION, SMTP, AND EXCHANGE SERVER 2007

This lab contains the following exercises and activities:

Exercise 1.1	Configuring Your Lab Computers
Exercise 1.2	Testing Email Server Name Resolution
Exercise 1.3	Testing SMTP Support
Exercise 1.4	Researching Exchange Server 2007 Features

Lab Review Questions

BEFORE YOU BEGIN

Lab 1 assumes that setup has been completed as specified in the setup document and that your workstation has connectivity to the classroom network and other lab computers.

To perform the exercises in this lab manual, you will need to have three fully updated instances of Windows Server 2003 SP2 Enterprise Edition or later installed. Although these instances can be installed on different computers, it is assumed that these instances will be hosted by three different virtual machines on the same computer using virtualization software such as Microsoft Virtual PC, Microsoft Virtual Server, VMWare Server, or VMWare Workstation. This will allow you to interface with all three instances of Windows Server 2003 SP2 from the same computer during the exercises.

For simplicity, the Administrator account on each instance of Windows Server 2003 SP2 should have the same password. In addition, each instance of Windows Server 2003 SP2 will have a different computer name: StudentXX-A, StudentXX-B, and StudentXX-C, where XX is a unique number assigned to you by your instructor. Each instance of Windows Server 2003 SP2 will need to have a single network interface configured with a unique IP address as well as a subnet mask and default gateway necessary for Internet access within the classroom. The network interface on StudentXX-A should also be configured with the DNS server used for Internet access within the classroom. The DNS server configured within the network interfaces on StudentXX-B and StudentXX-C should be the IP address of StudentXX-A.

Figure 1-1 provides an example configuration for three instances of Windows Server 2003 on the first student computer using the 10.0.0.0 network, a classroom default gateway of 10.0.0.254, and a classroom DNS server of 10.0.0.253.

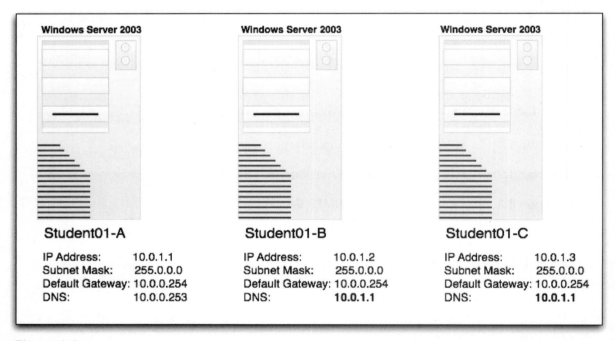

Figure 1-1
A sample Student01 computer with three virtual machines

Obtain your unique student number as well as the IP configuration used within your classroom for Internet access from your instructor.

Next, fill in the appropriate name and IP configuration for your computer in Figure 1-2 using the space provided. You can use this information for future reference.

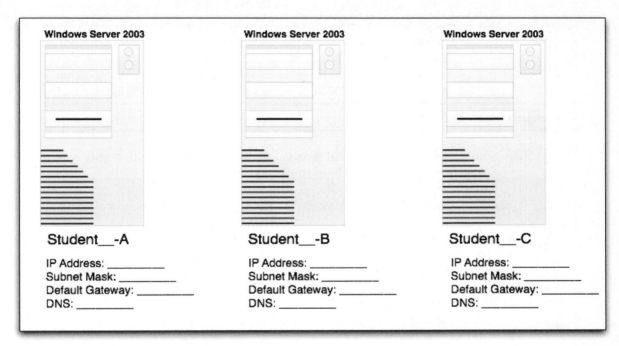

Figure 1-2
Your computer and virtual machine configuration

> NOTE
>
> *In this lab, you will see the characters XX. When you see these characters, substitute the two-digit number assigned to your computer.*

SCENARIO

You are the network administrator for your organization. Before implementing Active Directory and Exchange Server 2007 within your organization, you wish to investigate how DNS and SMTP work to relay email as well as explore the structure and features within Exchange Server 2007.

After completing this lab, you will be able to:

- Perform DNS name resolution using A and MX records

- Determine SMTP support on an email server

- Understand Exchange Server 2007 structure and features

Estimated lab time: 60 minutes

Exercise 1.1	Configuring Your Lab Computers
Overview	Before performing the exercises in this lab manual, you must ensure that the three instances of Windows Server 2003 are configured according to the information that you supplied earlier in Figure 1-2. To complete this lab exercise, StudentXX-A, StudentXX-B, and StudentXX-C must be started.
Completion time	20 minutes

1. On StudentXX-A, log in as Administrator. Your instructor will supply you with the appropriate password for the administrator account.

2. Click Start, Control Panel, Network Connections, and then click your network connection.

3. At the network connection status window, click Properties. When the network connection properties window appears, highlight Internet Protocol (TCP/IP) and click Properties.

4. Supply the appropriate IP address, subnet mask, default gateway, and DNS server (Preferred DNS Server) that you recorded for StudentXX-A in Figure 1-2.

5. Click OK to close the Internet Protocol (TCP/IP) Properties window, click OK to close the network connection properties, and click Close to close your network connection status window.

6. Click Start, Control Panel, and then click System. When the System Properties window appears, highlight the Computer Name tab and click Change.

7. Type the appropriate computer name in the Computer name dialog box (StudentXX-A from Figure 1-2) and click OK. Click OK to close System Properties and click OK again when warned that you must restart your computer. Click Yes to restart StudentXX-A.

8. On StudentXX-B, log in as Administrator. Your instructor will supply you with the appropriate password for the administrator account.

9. Click Start, Control Panel, Network Connections, and then click your network connection.

10. At the network connection status window, click Properties. When the network connection properties window appears, highlight Internet Protocol (TCP/IP) and click Properties.

11. Supply the appropriate IP address, subnet mask, default gateway, and DNS server (Preferred DNS Server) that you recorded for StudentXX-B in Figure 1-2.

12. Click OK to close the Internet Protocol (TCP/IP) Properties window, click OK to close the network connection properties, and click Close to close your network connection status window.

13. Click Start, Control Panel, and then click System. When the System Properties window appears, highlight the Computer Name tab and click Change.

14. Type the appropriate computer name in the Computer name dialog box (StudentXX-B from Figure 1-2) and click OK. Click OK to close System Properties and click OK again when warned that you must restart your computer. Click Yes to restart StudentXX-B. After StudentXX-B has restarted, log in as Administrator and shut down StudentXX-B.

15. On StudentXX-C, log in as Administrator. Your instructor will supply you with the appropriate password for the administrator account.

16. Click Start, Control Panel, Network Connections, and then click your network connection.

17. At the network connection status window, click Properties. When the network connection properties window appears, highlight Internet Protocol (TCP/IP) and click Properties.

18. Supply the appropriate IP address, subnet mask, default gateway, and DNS server (Preferred DNS Server) that you recorded for StudentXX-C in Figure 1-2.

19. Click OK to close the Internet Protocol (TCP/IP) Properties window, click OK to close the network connection properties, and click Close to close your network connection status window.

20. Click Start, Control Panel, and then click System. When the System Properties window appears, highlight the Computer Name tab and click Change.

21. Type the appropriate computer name in the Computer name dialog box (StudentXX-C from Figure 1-2) and click OK. Click OK to close System Properties and click OK again when warned that you must restart your computer. Click Yes to restart StudentXX-C. After StudentXX-C has restarted, log in as Administrator and shut down StudentXX-C.

Exercise 1.2	Testing Email Server Name Resolution
Overview	In the following exercise, you run the appropriate commands to resolve DNS A and MX records.
	To complete this lab exercise, StudentXX-A must be started and have Internet access.
Completion time	10 minutes

1. On StudentXX-A, log in as Administrator.

2. Click Start, All Programs, Accessories, and then click Command Prompt to open a command prompt window.

3. Type **nslookup** at the command prompt and press Enter.

4. At the nslookup prompt, type **www.hotmail.com** and press Enter to resolve the DNS A record for the www.hotmail.com web server.

Question 1	How many IP addresses does www.hotmail.com resolve to?

Question 2	If there are multiple IP addresses for www.hotmail.com, which IP address will be used and what DNS feature will be used to load balance their usage?

5. At the nslookup prompt, type **set q=mx** and press Enter to configure nslookup to view MX records on future queries.

6. At the nslookup prompt, type **www.hotmail.com** and press Enter.

Question 3	What other command can be used in place of set q=mx to achieve the same result?

Question 4	Why were no MX records displayed?

7. At the nslookup prompt, type **hotmail.com** and press Enter. The nslookup utility will return the MX record(s) and associated A record(s) for the hotmail.com domain.

8. Repeat the previous step several times.

Question 5	How many MX records are displayed?

Question 6	Do these MX records have the same priority number?

Question 7	If the MX records have the same priority number, which record will be used first and what DNS feature will be used to load balance their usage?

Question 8	If the MX records do not have the same priority number, which record will be used first and why is this useful?

Question 9	How many A records are displayed for each MX record?

Question 10	*After your computer selects the appropriate MX record, which A record will it use and what DNS feature will be used to load balance their usage?*

Question 11	*Does the order of MX and A records change? If so, what feature of DNS is responsible for the reordering?*

9. Write down the IP address of the first hotmail.com email server for use in the next exercise: _____

10. Type **exit** at the nslookup prompt and press Enter to close the nslookup utility.

11. Close the command prompt window.

Exercise 1.3   Testing SMTP Support

Overview	In the following exercise, you will use the telnet utility to verify SMTP support on an email server.
	To complete this lab exercise, StudentXX-A must be started and have Internet access.
Completion time	5 minutes

1. On StudentXX-A, log in as Administrator.

2. Click Start, All Programs, Accessories, and then click Command Prompt to open a command prompt window.

3. Type **telnet *IP_address* 25** at the command prompt (where ***IP_address*** is the IP address of a hotmail.com email server that you recorded in Step 9 of the previous exercise) and press Enter. If successful, you should see a banner that indicates the name and legal disclaimer for the hotmail.com email server. If unsuccessful, your Internet connection is blocking traffic on port 25 with a firewall and you will be unable to perform the following steps using the hotmail.com email server. In this case, your instructor can supply you with the IP address of an existing classroom email server that you can use in place of IP_address to complete the following steps.

4. Type **EHLO** at the command prompt and press Enter. Note the Hello response given.

Question 12	*Given the response, what version of SMTP does the hotmail.com email server support?*

Question 13	*What do the lines that start with 250 indicate?*

5. Type **HELLO** at the command prompt and press Enter. Note the Hello response given.

Question 14	Given the response, what version of SMTP does the hotmail.com email server support?

6. Type **quit** at the command prompt and press Enter.

7. Close the command prompt window.

Exercise 1.4 Researching Exchange Server 2007 Features	
Overview	In the following exercise, you use the Microsoft Technet Web site to research Exchange Server 2007 features and server roles.
	To complete this lab exercise, StudentXX-A must be started and have Internet access.
Completion time	15 minutes

1. On StudentXX-A, log in as Administrator.

2. Navigate to the installation media for Exchange Server 2007 and double click on the **setup.exe** file.

3. At the Welcome screen, click **Read about Microsoft Exchange Server 2007 SP1**. Your web browser will open and connect you to the appropriate information about Exchange Server 2007 SP1 at technet.microsoft.com.

4. Review the descriptions of the features and server roles available in Exchange Server 2007.

5. When finished, close your web browser and any other open windows.

LAB REVIEW QUESTIONS

Completion time   10 minutes

1. Describe what you learned by completing this lab.

2. How does the DNS round-robin feature load balance connections when there are more than one MX or associated A record to describe email servers for a domain?

3. Which version of SMTP (ESMTP or legacy SMTP) will be used first when an email server initiates a connection to another email server and why?

LAB 2
WORKING WITH ACTIVE DIRECTORY

This lab contains the following exercises and activities:

Exercise 2.1	Installing a New Forest and Domain
Exercise 2.2	Installing an Additional Domain Controller
Exercise 2.3	Raising the Domain and Forest Functional Level
Exercise 2.4	Configuring Sites and Replication
Exercise 2.5	Configuring Global Catalog and UGMC
Exercise 2.6	Viewing and Configuring FSMO Roles
Exercise 2.7	Creating and Managing Active Directory Objects
Lab Review Questions	
Lab Challenge 2.1	Seizing an FSMO Role
Lab Challenge 2.2	Configuring a Cross Forest Trust Relationship

BEFORE YOU BEGIN

Lab 2 assumes that setup has been completed as specified in the setup document and that StudentXX-A, StudentXX-B, and StudentXX-C have been configured according to the exercises in Lab 1. Moreover, StudentXX-A, StudentXX-B, and StudentXX-C must have connectivity to the classroom network and the Internet.

> **NOTE**
>
> *In this lab, you will see the characters XX. When you see these characters, substitute the two-digit number assigned to your computer.*

SCENARIO

Your organization must deploy two domain controllers in its head office location. Although plans have been made to implement a branch office location, domain controllers will be deployed in the branch office at a later time. You must install and configure an Active Directory (AD) forest and domain in your head office location that supports Exchange Server 2007 and the expected configuration of your branch office. Moreover, your forest and domain should have multiple Global Catalog servers; fault tolerance for Flexible Single Master Operations (FSMO) roles; and should contain the appropriate organizational unit (OU), user, group, and computer objects.

In the Lab Challenge, you are asked to seize an FSMO role and create a trust relationship to another forest.

After completing this lab, you will be able to:

- ■ Install Active Directory forests and domains

- ■ View and change domain and forest functional levels

- ■ View and configure Global Catalog and Universal Group Membership Caching

- ■ View and change domain- and forestwide FSMO roles

- ■ Create and manage Active Directory objects such as OUs, users, groups, and computers

- ■ Create trust relationships

Estimated lab time: 260 minutes

Exercise 2.1	Installing a New Forest and Domain
Overview	In the following exercise, you install Active Directory on StudentXX-A as the first domain controller in a new forest. Before running the Active Directory installation wizard, you must first ensure StudentXX-A is configured to use itself for DNS name resolution. Following installation, you will verify the creation of SRV records, reconfigure DNS to forward external name resolution requests to the classroom DNS server, as well as enable DNS aging and scavenging.

To complete this lab exercise, StudentXX-A must be started and have network access. |
| Completion time | 60 minutes |

1. On StudentXX-A, log in as Administrator.

2. Click Start, Control Panel, Network Connections, and then click your network connection.

3. At the network connection status window, click Properties. When the network connection properties window appears, highlight Internet Protocol (TCP/IP) and click Properties.

4. Enter **127.0.0.1** in the Preferred DNS server dialog box. This will ensure that the Active Directory installation program will use StudentXX-A for DNS name resolution (and install the DNS service as a result).

5. Click Start, and then click Run. In the Run dialog box, type **dcpromo** and press Enter.

6. When the Active Directory Installation Wizard appears, click Next.

7. At the Operating System Compatibility page, click Next.

8. At the Domain Controller Type page, ensure that **Domain controller for a new domain** is selected and click Next.

9. At the Create New Domain page, ensure that **Domain in a new forest** is selected and click Next.

10. At the New Domain Name page, enter **StudentXX.com** as the DNS name of the first domain in the forest. Click Next when finished.

11. At the NetBIOS Domain Name page, review the NetBIOS name generated from your domain DNS name and click Next.

12. At the Database and Log Folders page, review the default location for the AD database and database logs and click Next.

Question 1	What file system must be used for the AD database and Logs?

13. At the Shared System Volume page, review the default location for the SYSVOL shared folder and click Next.

Question 2	What file system must be used for the SYSVOL shared folder?

14. At the DNS Registration Diagnostics page, ensure that **Install and configure the DNS server on this computer** is selected and click Next.

15. At the Permissions page, ensure that **Permissions compatible with Windows 2000 or Windows Server 2003 operating systems** is selected and click Next.

16. At the Directory Services Restore Mode Administrator Password page, enter **Secret123** in both password dialog boxes, and click Next.

> **Question 3**
>
> *When is the directory service restore mode password used?*

17. At the Summary page, review your installation choices and click Next. Insert your Windows Server 2003 CD when prompted.

18. After the installation has completed, click the Finish button. Click **Restart Now** when prompted to restart your domain controller.

19. After StudentXX-A has restarted, log in to your domain as Administrator.

20. Click Start, All Programs, Administrative Tools, and then click DNS.

21. In the DNS console, expand the Forward Lookup Zones folder under StudentXX-A and highlight StudentXX.com. You should see several folders that contain SRV records used by Active Directory.

> **Question 4**
>
> *What service should you restart on your domain controller if SRV records have not been automatically created within DNS?*

22. Right click StudentXX.com and click Properties.

23. In the Dynamic updates drop-down box, select **Nonsecure and secure**. This will allow your Edge role server (StudentXX-C) to create DNS records using dynamic update without being a member of the domain.

24. Click Aging and select **Scavenge stale resource records**. Click OK. Click OK again to close StudentXX.com properties.

> **Question 5**
>
> *Why should you enable DNS aging and scavenging on a DNS zone used for Active Directory?*

25. Right click StudentXX-A in the DNS console and click Properties.

26. Highlight the Forwarders tab, select **All other DNS domains** and enter the IP address of classroom DNS server in the **Selected domain's forwarder IP address list** section. Click Add and click OK. This will ensure that any DNS name resolution requests that are not within the StudentXX.com domain will be forwarded to the classroom DNS server.

27. Close the DNS console.

Exercise 2.2   Installing an Additional Domain Controller

Overview	In the following exercise, you install Active Directory on StudentXX-B as the second domain controller in an existing domain in an existing forest. Before running the Active Directory installation wizard, you must first ensure StudentXX-B is configured to use StudentXX-A for DNS name resolution (as configured in Exercise 2.1).
	To complete this lab exercise, StudentXX-A and StudentXX-B must be started and have network access.
Completion time	40 minutes

1. On StudentXX-B, log in as Administrator.

2. Click Start, and then click Run. In the Run dialog box, type **dcpromo** and press Enter.

3. When the Active Directory Installation Wizard appears, click Next.

4. At the Operating System Compatibility page, click Next.

5. At the Domain Controller Type page, ensure that **Additional domain controller for an existing domain** is selected and click Next.

6. At the Network Credentials page, enter the username and password for the Administrator account on StudentXX-A (which is now the domain Administrator account) and enter **StudentXX.com** as the domain.

7. At the Additional Domain Controller page, ensure that StudentXX.com is listed as the DNS name of the existing domain in the forest. Click Next when finished.

8. At the Database and Log Folders page, review the default location for the AD database and database logs and click Next.

9. At the Shared System Volume page, review the default location for the SYSVOL shared folder and click Next.

10. At the Directory Services Restore Mode Administrator Password page, enter **Secret123** in both password dialog boxes and click Next.

11. At the Summary page, review your installation choices and click Next.

12. After the installation has completed, click the Finish button. Click **Restart Now** when prompted to restart your domain controller.

Exercise 2.3	Raising the Domain and Forest Functional Level
Overview	In the following exercise, you will raise the domain and forest functional level to Windows Server 2003 to gain the most functionality from your Active Directory infrastructure as well as prepare for the implementation of Exchange Server 2007.
	To complete this lab exercise, StudentXX-A and StudentXX-B must be started and have network access.
Completion time	5 minutes

1.   On StudentXX-A, log in as Administrator.

2.   Click Start, Administrative Tools, and Active Directory Domains and Trusts. The Active Directory Domains and Trusts console appears.

3.   In the left pane, right click StudentXX.com and select **Raise Domain Functional Level** from the menu.

4.   At the Raise Domain Functional Level window, select **Windows Server 2003** from the drop-down box and click Raise.

5.   Click OK to confirm the action.

6.   Click OK again to close the Raise Domain Functional Level dialog box.

7.   In the left pane, right click **Active Directory Domains and Trusts** and select **Raise Forest Functional Level** from the menu.

8.   At the Raise Forest Functional Level window, select **Windows Server 2003** from the drop-down box and click Raise.

9.   Click OK to confirm the action.

10.   Click OK again to close the Raise Domain Functional Level dialog box.

11.   Close the Active Directory Domains and Trusts console.

Question 6	*What other utility may be used to raise your domain functional level?*

Exercise 2.4	Configuring Sites and Replication
Overview	StudentXX-A and StudentXX-B are in the same AD site at the head office of your organization. However, you will soon be implementing a branch office that will maintain its own domain controllers in the future. The branch office will have a low-bandwidth Internet connection and will use the 44.92.0.0 network. As a result, you should only replicate between domain

controllers in the head office and branch office on an hourly basis during
nonworking hours (working hours are 8:00 a.m. to 6:00 p.m.). To support
this configuration, you will need to configure different site and subnet
objects for your head office and branch office as well as configure a site link
object that restricts replication between sites to meet your organization's
needs. Moreover, StudentXX-B has a faster network interface and should
be configured as the bridgehead server for any inter-site replication for the
head office site.

Although you will not be configuring an additional domain controller in the
branch office site during this exercise, it is assumed that it will be
performed in the future. In this exercise, you will prepare the site
infrastructure for the branch office and configure future replication between
the head office and branch office site.

To complete this lab exercise, StudentXX-A and StudentXX-B must be
started and have network access.

Completion time	30 minutes

1. On StudentXX-A, log in as Administrator.

2. Click Start, Administrative Tools, and Active Directory Sites and Services. The Active Directory Sites and Services console appears.

3. In the left pane, expand Default-First-Site-Name. Underneath Default-First-Site-Name, expand the Servers folder.

Question 7	What server objects exist under the Servers folder and why?

Question 8	When a change is made to the Active Directory database on StudentXX-A or StudentXX-B, when will those changes replicate to the other domain controller and why?

4. Expand StudentXX-B and then expand NTDS Settings. Right click the connection object in the right pane and select Replicate Now to manually initiate replication.

5. Right click Default-First-Site-Name in the left pane and select Rename from the menu. Type **HeadOffice** beside the site object and press Enter.

6. Right click the Sites folder and select New Site from the menu.

7. At the New Object—Site window, type **BranchOffice** in the Name dialog box. Next, click on DEFAULTIPSITELINK to ensure that the new site uses the default site link object and click OK.

8. Right click the Subnets folder and select New Subnet from the menu.

9. At the New Object—Subnet window, type the IP network used by StudentXX-A and StudentXX-B in the Address dialog box and the associated subnet mask in the Mask dialog box.

10. Highlight the HeadOffice site and click OK.

11. Again, right click the Subnets folder and select New Subnet from the menu. In the Address dialog box, enter the IP network **44.92.0.0**. In the Mask dialog box, enter the subnet mask **255.255.0.0**. Next, highlight the BranchOffice site and click OK.

Question 9	When a new domain controller with a network interface on the 44.92.0.0 network is added to the domain, what site will it be automatically added to and why?

12. In the left pane, expand Inter-Site Transports and highlight the IP folder. Note the DEFAULTIPSITELINK object within the IP folder.

13. Right click the DEFAULTIPSITELINK object in the right page and select Delete from the menu. When prompted to confirm the deletion, click Yes.

14. Right click the IP folder in the left pane and select New Site Link from the menu.

15. At the New Object—Site Link window, type **HeadOffice-to-BranchOffice** in the Name dialog box. Ensure that the HeadOffice and BranchOffice sites are included within the site link (they must be located in the right selection box) and click OK.

16. Right click the HeadOffice-to-BranchOffice site link in the right pane and select Properties from the menu.

17. At the site link property window, enter **60** in the Replicate every dialog box and click the Change Schedule button.

18. At the Schedule window, highlight the cells that indicate 8:00 a.m. to 6:00 p.m. Monday to Friday, choose Replication Not Available, and click OK. Click OK to close the site link property window.

Question 10	When a change is made to the Active Directory database on StudentXX-A or StudentXX-B, when will those changes replicate to domain controllers in the BranchOffice site and why?

19. In the left pane, expand the HeadOffice site, and expand the Servers folder. Right click ServerXX-B and select Properties.

20. Highlight IP in the left dialog box and click the **Add** >> button to move it to the right dialog box. This will ensure that ServerXX-B is used as the bridgehead server for the HeadOffice site.

21. Click OK to close the ServerXX-B Properties screen.

Question 11	*When a change is made to the Active Directory database on StudentXX-A, what path will it take to replicate to the domain controllers in the BranchOffice site and why?*

22. Close the Active Directory Sites and Services console.

Exercise 2.5   Configuring Global Catalog and UGMC

Overview	From your research, you know that Exchange Server 2007 communicates frequently with the Global Catalog. Since you plan to deploy Exchange Server 2007 within your HeadOffice site, you wish to enable the Global Catalog on both of the domain controllers within the HeadOffice site (StudentXX-A and StudentXX-B). Due to bandwidth concerns surrounding the replication of the Global Catalog, you will not deploy the Global Catalog on any domain controllers in the BranchOffice site. However, to speed domain logons, you plan to enable Universal Group Membership Caching (UGMC) on the BranchOffice site.
	To complete this lab exercise, StudentXX-A and StudentXX-B must be started and have network access.
Completion time	5 minutes

1. On StudentXX-A, log in as Administrator.

2. Click Start, Administrative Tools, and Active Directory Sites and Services. The Active Directory Sites and Services console appears.

3. In the left pane, expand the HeadOffice site, expand the Servers folder, and expand StudentXX-A to expose the NTDS Settings object. Right click NTDS Settings and select Properties from the menu. View the Global Catalog check box.

Question 12	*Is StudentXX-A a Global Catalog server and why?*

4. Click OK to close the NTDS Settings Properties screen.

5. In the left pane, expand the HeadOffice site, expand the Servers folder, and expand StudentXX-B to expose the NTDS Settings object. Right click NTDS Settings and select Properties from the menu. View the Global Catalog check box.

Question 13	*Is StudentXX-B a Global Catalog server and why?*

6. Place a check mark in the Global Catalog checkbox and click OK to close the NTDS Settings Properties screen.

7. In the left pane, highlight the BranchOffice site. In the right pane, right click NTDS Site Settings and select Properties from the menu.

8. Place a check mark in the Enable Universal Group Membership Caching checkbox and click OK to close the NTDS Site Settings Properties screen.

Exercise 2.6	Viewing and Configuring FSMO Roles
Overview	In your Active Directory forest and domain, you wish to distribute the available FSMO roles to ensure that the failure of a single domain controller does not take all FSMO roles offline. As a result, you have decided to place the schema master, PDC emulator, and RID master FSMO roles on StudentXX-A, and place the domain naming and infrastructure master FSMO roles on StudentXX-B. To complete this lab exercise, StudentXX-A and StudentXX-B must be started and have network access.
Completion time	15 minutes

1. On StudentXX-B, log in as Administrator.

2. Click Start, Run, and type **regsvr32 schmmgmt.dll** in the Run box to register the Active Directory Schema snap-in. Click OK to close the RegSvr32 window.

3. Next, click Start, Run, type **mmc** in the Run box and press Enter to open the Microsoft Management Console (MMC).

4. In the MMC, click File and select Add/Remove Snap-in. At the Add/Remove Snap-in window, click Add and select Active Directory Schema from the Add Standalone Snap-in window. Click Add and then click Close to close the Add Standalone Snap-in window.

5. Click OK in the Add/Remove Snap-in to add the Active Directory Schema to the MMC.

6. In the left pane of the MMC, expand Active Directory Schema. Next, right click Active Directory Schema and select Operations Master from the menu.

7. At the Change Schema Master window, observe the name of the domain controller that currently holds the Schema Master FSMO role.

Question 14	Which domain controller currently holds the schema master FSMO and why?

8. Click Close to close the Change Schema Master window.

9. Close the MMC window. When prompted to save your MMC settings, click No.

10. Click Start, Administrative Tools, and Active Directory Domains and Trusts.

11. In the left pane of the Active Directory Domains and Trusts console, right click Active Directory Domains and Trusts and select Connect to Domain Controller from the menu.

12. At the Connect to Domain Controller window, select StudentXX-B from the list and click OK to close the Connect to Domain Controller window.

13. In the left pane of the Active Directory Domains and Trusts console, right click Active Directory Domains and Trusts and select Operations Master from the menu.

14. At the Change Operations Master window, observe the name of the domain controller that currently holds the Domain Naming Master FSMO role.

Question 15	Which domain controller currently holds the domain naming master FSMO and why?

15. Click the Change button to transfer the domain naming master to StudentXX-B. Click Yes when prompted to confirm the change.

16. Click Close to close the Change Operations Master window.

17. Close the Active Directory Domains and Trusts console.

18. Click Start, Administrative Tools, and Active Directory Users and Computers.

19. In the left pane of the Active Directory Users and Computers console, right click StudentXX.com and select Connect to Domain Controller from the menu.

20. At the Connect to Domain Controller window, select StudentXX-B from the list and click OK to close the Connect to Domain Controller window.

21. In the left pane, right click StudentXX.com and select Operations Masters from the menu.

22. At the Operations Master window, highlight each of the three tabs to observe the name of the domain controller that currently holds the RID master, PDC emulator, and infrastructure master FSMO roles.

Question 16	Which domain controller currently holds the RID master, PDC emulator, and infrastructure master FSMO roles and why?

23. Highlight the Infrastructure tab and click Change to transfer the infrastructure master role to StudentXX-B. Click Yes when prompted to confirm the change.

24. Click Close to close the Operations Master window.

25. Close the Active Directory Users and Computers console.

Exercise 2.7	Creating and Managing Active Directory Objects
Overview	In this exercise, you will create new OU, user, group, and computer objects. In addition, you will disable and reset user accounts as well as add user accounts to groups. Moreover, you will disable and reset a computer account. To complete this lab exercise, StudentXX-A and StudentXX-B must be started and have network access.
Completion time	60 minutes

1. On StudentXX-A, log in as Administrator.

2. Click Start, Administrative Tools, and Active Directory Users and Computers. The Active Directory Users and Computers console appears.

3. In the left pane, right click StudentXX.com and select New followed by Organizational Unit from the menu.

4. At the New Object—Organizational Unit window, type **Accounting** and click OK.

5. Use the procedure detailed in the previous two steps to create the **Marketing**, **Sales**, and **Production** organizational units (OUs) under your domain.

6. In the left pane, right click the Sales OU object and select New followed by User from the menu.

7. At the New Object—User window, type **Sophia** in the First name dialog box, **Boren** in the Last name dialog box, **sophia.boren** in the User logon name dialog box and click Next.

8. Type the password **Secret123** in both password dialog boxes. Next, deselect **User must change password at next logon** and select **User cannot change password** and **Password never expires**.

9. Click Next. Click Finish to create the user account.

10. In the right pane, right click the Sophia Boren user account and select Properties. Highlight the Organization tab, type **Sales** in the Department dialog box, and click OK.

11. Using the procedure detailed in Steps 6 to 10, create the other user accounts listed in Table 2-1 in the appropriate OUs with the appropriate Department attributes. Each user should have a logon name of **firstname.lastname** (lowercase).

Table 2-1
User Account Information

User Name	OU/Department
Sophia Boren	Sales
Mel Booker	Accounting
Celine DeVries	Accounting
Mike Moritz	Marketing
Mark Daly	Production
Tiger Smith	Accounting
Meg Roombas	Sales
Jacques Guillere	Sales
Juan Ton	Marketing
Sarah Parkers	Production
Lois Lipshitz	Production
Jessica Augustus	Accounting
Tom Hurt	Production
Bernadette Jones	Production
Jennifer Coupland	Production
Courtney Davies	Marketing
Lisa Lackner	Sales
Mathew Kropf	Production
Matt Adams	Sales
David Schwan	Production

12. In the left pane, right click StudentXX.com and select New followed by Group from the menu.

13. At the New Object—Group window, type **Managers** in the Group name dialog box and ensure that Global is selected in the Group scope section and Security is selected in the Group Type section. Click OK when finished.

14. Use the procedure detailed in the previous two steps to create the **Executives** and **Supervisors** groups under your domain.

Question 17	Why should the group scope be Global for the groups that you created?

15. In the left pane, highlight the Sales OU. Next, right click the Sophia Boren user account in the right pane and select Properties. Highlight the Members tab of the group's properties.

16. Click the Add button. In the Select Users, Contacts, Computers, or Groups window, click Advanced, and then click the Find Now button. Select the Managers group and click OK to return to the Select Users, Contacts, Computers, or Groups window.

17. Click OK to return to the group properties window. Click OK to modify the group membership.

Question 18	What other method may be used to add members to a group?

18. Use the procedure detailed in the previous three steps to assign the appropriate users to the correct groups as described in Table 2-2.

Table 2-2
User Group Information

User Name	Group
Sophia Boren	Managers
Mel Booker	Supervisors
Celine DeVries	Executives
Mike Moritz	Managers
Mark Daly	Supervisors
Tiger Smith	Managers
Meg Roombas	Supervisors
Jacques Guillere	Executives
Juan Ton	Managers
Sarah Parkers	Supervisors
Lois Lipshitz	Supervisors
Jessica Augustus	Executives
Tom Hurt	Managers
Bernadette Jones	Managers
Jennifer Coupland	Supervisors
Courtney Davies	Executives
Lisa Lackner	Managers
Mathew Kropf	Supervisors
Matt Adams	Executives
David Schwan	Supervisors

19. In the left pane, highlight the Production OU. Next, right click the Lois Lipshitz user account in the right pane and select Disable. Click OK at the confirmation window.

20. In the left pane, highlight the Accounting OU. Next, right click the Tiger Smith user account in the right pane and select Reset Password. Type **Secret123** in both password dialog boxes and click OK.

Question 19	When would you normally reset a user's password and what should you do prior to this procedure?

21. In the left pane, right click the Accounting OU and select New followed by Computer from the menu.

22. At the New Object—Computer window, type **Client1** in the Computer name dialog box. Ensure that Domain Admins will be allowed to join the computer with the NetBIOS name Client1 to the domain and click Next. Click Next and then click Finish to create the computer account.

Question 20	You have just created a computer account that can be used later when a client computer with the NetBIOS name of Client1 is joined to the domain. What is this process called?

23. Right click the Client1 computer account and select Reset Account. Click Yes to confirm the reset operation.

Question 21	When would you normally reset a computer account?

Question 22	What must you do on the client computer after resetting a computer account?

24. Right click the Client1 computer account and select Disable Account. Click Yes to confirm the reset operation and click OK to close the confirmation window.

Question 23	Will any domain user be able to log in to the domain using the Client1 computer?

25. Close the Active Directory Users and Computers console.

LAB REVIEW QUESTIONS

Completion time	15 minutes

1. Describe what you learned by completing this lab.

2. If you deployed different domains for your branch and head offices, would you need to configure sites? Explain.

3. In Exercise 2.7, you configured the same password for each user account. Is this a good practice? Explain.

4. In Exercise 2.3, you raised your domain and forest functional levels to Windows Server 2003. What restrictions does this impose on your domain and forest?

5. Which FSMO role should be in the same site as your first Exchange server prior to Exchange server deployment?

6. Which group scope is stored in the Global Catalog?

7. In general, you should have at least one Global Catalog server in each site. If you are unable to place a Global Catalog server in a particular site, what should you enable on the site to support domain logons if the domain is at the Windows Server 2003 functional level?

LAB CHALLENGE 2.1: SEIZING AN FSMO ROLE

Completion time	15 minutes

Assume that StudentXX-B is experiencing intermittent hardware failure and is unable to service requests. As a result, you should seize any FSMO roles that StudentXX-B hosts from a working domain controller to ensure that your domain and forest function normally. Shut down StudentXX-B. Next, use the ntdsutil.exe utility on StudentXX-A to seize the domain naming and infrastructure master FSMO roles.

LAB CHALLENGE 2.2: CONFIGURING A CROSS FOREST TRUST RELATIONSHIP

Completion time	15 minutes

Your organization has recently merged with another organization. As a result, users within your organization require access to resources in the other organization and vice versa. To support this requirement, you plan to create a cross forest trust relationship between the two forests.

To perform this within the classroom, you will need to find a partner and create a cross forest trust relationship between your forest (StudentXX.com) and their forest (StudentYY.com).

<table>
<tr><td>HINT</td><td>Before you create a trust relationship, you must first ensure that your domain can resolve the SRV records for StudentYY.com. To do this, you will need to configure your DNS server and the DNS server in StudentYY.com. Open the DNS console in both forests, access the properties of your DNS server, highlight the Forwarders tab, and configure the appropriate information.</td></tr>
</table>

LAB 3
DEPLOYING EXCHANGE SERVER 2007 SP1

This lab contains the following exercises and activities:

Exercise 3.1   Deploying the First Exchange Server

Exercise 3.2   Deploying the Second Exchange Server

Exercise 3.3   Deploying the Third Exchange Server

Lab Review Questions

Lab Challenge 3.1   Performing an Unattended Exchange Server Installation

BEFORE YOU BEGIN

Lab 3 assumes that setup has been completed as specified in the setup document and that StudentXX-A, StudentXX-B, and StudentXX-C have connectivity to the classroom network and the Internet. Moreover, Lab 3 assumes that you have completed the exercises in previous labs.

> **NOTE**
>
> *In this lab, you will see the characters XX. When you see these characters, substitute the two-digit number assigned to your computer.*

SCENARIO

You plan to deploy Exchange Server 2007 SP1 Enterprise Edition within your organization. StudentXX-A will be the first Exchange server within the organization and host the Mailbox,

Hub, CAS, and UM roles. To provide fault tolerance and load balancing for the Mailbox, Hub, and CAS roles in the HeadOffice site, you will also install Exchange Server 2007 on StudentXX-B with the Mailbox, Hub, and CAS roles. To provide additional security and filtering for inbound and outbound Internet email, you will also install the Edge role on StudentXX-C. Figure 3-1 depicts the Exchange server roles that will be installed during this lab.

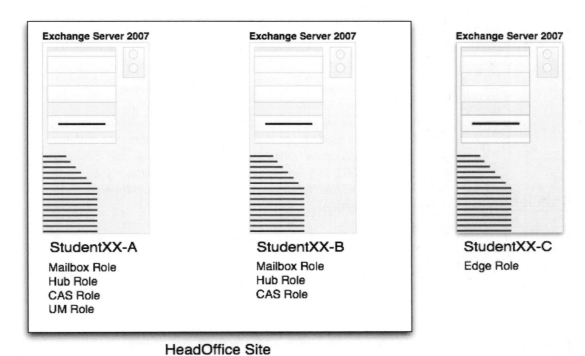

HeadOffice Site

Figure 3-1
Exchange server roles for StudentXX-A, StudentXX-B, and StudentXX-C

In the Lab Challenge, you will install the UM role on StudentXX-B using an unattended installation.

After completing this lab, you will be able to:

- Prepare a Windows Server 2003 computer for Exchange Server 2007 installation

- Install Exchange Server 2007 in different configurations

- Verify the installation of Exchange server roles

- Perform an unattended Exchange Server 2007 installation

Estimated lab time: 250 minutes

<table>
<tr><td rowspan="6" style="vertical-align:middle">NOTE</td><td>In Lab Exercises 3.1, 3.2, and 3.3, you will install Exchange Server 2007. Prior to each installation, you will need to install the necessary software prerequisites as well as prepare the Active Directory domain for Exchange Server 2007.</td></tr>
<tr><td>You can install the 32-bit or 64-bit version of Exchange Server 2007 SP1 Enterprise Edition in Lab Exercises 3.1, 3.2, and 3.3. However, if you wish to install the 64-bit version of Exchange Server 2007, you must have a 64-bit installation of Windows Server 2003.</td></tr>
<tr><td>After each installation, you will verify the installation of the server roles, view installation logs, and update Exchange Server 2007 using Microsoft Update. Although you would normally configure Automatic Updates or WSUS to perform continuous updates for your Windows Server 2003 operating system and Exchange Server 2007, this will use unnecessary bandwidth in the classroom. As a result, we will not be performing these actions in this exercise.</td></tr>
<tr><td>In a production environment, you would also enter an Exchange Server 2007 license key following installation. However, in Lab Exercises 3.1, 3.2, and 3.3, no license key is necessary because we will be using Exchange Server 2007 in evaluation mode throughout this lab manual.</td></tr>
</table>

Exercise 3.1   Deploying the First Exchange Server

Overview	In the following exercise, you will install Exchange Server 2007 SP1 Enterprise Edition on StudentXX-A with the Mailbox, Hub, CAS, and UM roles as depicted earlier in Figure 3-1.
	To complete this lab exercise, StudentXX-A and StudentXX-B must be started and have network access.
Completion time	100 minutes

1. On StudentXX-A, log in as Administrator.

2. Obtain and install the PowerShell 1.0, .NET Framework 2.0, .NET Framework 2.0 SP1, MMC Version 3.0, MSXML 6.0, Windows Media Encoder, and Windows Media Audio Voice Codec packages for your platform. You can download these packages for your platform from http://www.microsoft.com/downloads/.

3. Click Start, Control Panel, and then click Add or Remove Programs. At the Add or Remove Programs window, click Add/Remove Windows Components.

4. When the Windows Components Wizard window appears, place a checkmark beside Application Server. Next, highlight Application Server and click Details. In the Application Server window, place a checkmark beside ASP.NET and click OK.

Question 1	*Which IIS components must not be installed on a server that will run Exchange Server 2007?*

5. Highlight Networking Services and click Details. In the Networking Services window, place a checkmark beside RPC over HTTP Proxy and click OK.

Question 2	*Which server role requires the RPC over HTTP Proxy service?*

6. Press Next to install the components. Insert your Windows Server 2003 installation media when prompted and press OK. After the installation has finished, click Finish and close the Add or Remove Programs window.

7. Click Start, and then click Command Prompt. At the command prompt, navigate to the root of your Exchange Server 2007 installation media using the appropriate command at the command prompt. For example, if your installation media is identified as D drive in My Computer, type **D:** at the command prompt and press Enter.

8. Type **setup/PrepareLegacyExchangePermissions** at the command prompt and press Enter.

9. Type **setup/PrepareSchema** at the command prompt and press Enter.

10. Type **setup/PrepareAD/OrganizationName:StudentXXOrg** at the command prompt where XX is your unique student number and press Enter.

11. Type **setup/PrepareAllDomains** at the command prompt and press Enter.

12. Close the command prompt window.

13. Click Start and click My Computer. Navigate to the root of the Exchange Server 2007 media and double click the **setup.exe** file.

14. At the Exchange Server 2007 welcome screen, click **Step 4: Install Microsoft Exchange Server 2007 SP1**.

15. At the Exchange Server 2007 SP1 Setup wizard, click Next.

16. At the License Agreement page, select **I accept the terms in the license agreement** and click Next.

17. At the Error Reporting page, ensure that No is selected and click Next.

18. At the Installation Type page, select Custom Exchange Server Installation and click Next.

Question 3	What server roles and components are installed if you select Typical Exchange Server Installation from the Installation Type page?

19. At the Server Role Selection page, select **Mailbox Role**, **Client Access Role**, **Hub Transport Role**, **Unified Messaging Server Role**, and **Management Tools**. Click Next.

20. At the Client Settings page, select Yes to allow Entourage and Outlook 2003 and earlier MAPI clients access to your Exchange server and click Next.

Question 4	What will be automatically created on your Mailbox role after selecting Yes in the previous step?

21. Review the Readiness Checks page for any errors or warnings. If you have not met the proper software, hardware, and AD requirements, the Readiness Checks page will display errors that describe the component that must be installed or the action that must be taken before you are allowed to continue the Exchange Server 2007 installation. You must then install these components or perform the necessary actions and click Retry to perform the readiness checks again.

22. Click the Install button to begin the Exchange Server 2007 installation. At the end of the Exchange Server 2007 installation, deselect **Finalize installation using the Exchange Management Console** and click Finish. Click OK to close the information window and reboot StudentXX-A.

23. After StudentXX-A has rebooted, log in as Administrator.

24. Click Start, All Programs, Microsoft Exchange Server 2007, and then click Exchange Management Console. Click OK to close the dialog box stating that you have unlicensed servers.

25. Highlight Server Configuration in the console tree pane and view StudentXX-A in the detail pane. The Role column lists the roles that were successfully installed.

26. Close the Exchange Management Console.

27. Click Start, All Programs, Microsoft Exchange Server 2007, and then click Exchange Management Shell. The Exchange Management Shell window appears.

28. At the command prompt, type **get-ExchangeServer | Format-List** and press Enter to view your installed server roles.

29. Type **Get-SetupLog %systemroot%\ExchangeSetupLogs\ExchangeSetup.log–error–tree** and press Enter. Once the log file has been parsed, view the results.

30. Type **Get-SetupLog %systemroot%\ExchangeSetupLogs\ExchangeSetup.msilog–error–tree** and press Enter. Once the log file has been parsed, view the results.

31. Close the Exchange Management Shell.

32. Click Start and click My Computer. Navigate to the root of the Exchange Server 2007 media and double click the **setup.exe** file. After a few moments, the Exchange Server 2007 welcome screen appears.

33. Click **Step 5: Get Critical Updates for Microsoft Exchange**. Internet Explorer opens and directs you to the Microsoft Update Web site. Follow the instructions on the Web site to scan for and apply any critical updates that are required by your version of Exchange Server 2007.

34. Close all windows on your desktop.

Exercise 3.2	Deploying the Second Exchange Server
Overview	In the following exercise, you will install Exchange Server 2007 SP1 Enterprise Edition on StudentXX-B with the Mailbox, Hub, and CAS roles as depicted earlier in Figure 3-1.
	To complete this lab exercise, StudentXX-A and StudentXX-B must be started and have network access.
Completion time	60 minutes

1. On StudentXX-B, log in as Administrator.

2. Obtain and install the PowerShell 1.0, .NET Framework 2.0, .NET Framework 2.0 SP1, and MMC Version 3.0 packages for your platform. You can download these packages for your platform from http://www.microsoft.com/downloads/.

3. Click Start, Control Panel, and then click Add or Remove Programs. At the Add or Remove Programs window, click Add/Remove Windows Components.

4. When the Windows Components Wizard window appears, place a checkmark beside Application Server. Next, highlight Application Server and click Details. In the Application Server window, place a checkmark beside ASP.NET and click OK.

5. Highlight Networking Services and click Details. In the Networking Services window, place a checkmark beside RPC over HTTP Proxy and click OK.

Question 5	*Which additional Windows components are required by the Hub role?*

6. Press Next to install the components. Insert your Windows Server 2003 installation media when prompted and press OK. After the installation has finished, click Finish and close the Add or Remove Programs window.

7. Click Start and click My Computer. Navigate to the root of the Exchange Server 2007 media and double click the **setup.exe** file.

8. At the Exchange Server 2007 welcome screen, click **Step 4: Install Microsoft Exchange Server 2007 SP1**.

9. At the Exchange Server 2007 SP1 Setup wizard, click Next.

10. At the License Agreement page, select **I accept the terms in the license agreement** and click Next.

11. At the Error Reporting page, ensure that No is selected and click Next.

12. At the Installation Type page, select Custom Exchange Server Installation and click Next.

13. At the Server Role Selection page, select **Mailbox Role**, **Client Access Role**, **Hub Transport Role**, and **Management Tools**. Click Next.

14. At the Client Settings page, select Yes to allow Entourage and Outlook 2003 and earlier MAPI clients access to your Exchange server and click Next.

15. Review the Readiness Checks page for any errors or warnings. If you have not met the proper software, hardware, and AD requirements, the Readiness Checks page will display errors that describe the component that must be installed or the action that must be taken before you are allowed to continue the Exchange Server 2007 installation. You must then install these components or perform the necessary actions and click Retry to perform the readiness checks again.

16. Click the Install button to begin the Exchange Server 2007 installation. At the end of the Exchange Server 2007 installation, deselect **Finalize installation using the Exchange Management Console** and click Finish. Click OK to close the information window and reboot StudentXX-B.

17. After StudentXX-B has rebooted, log in as Administrator.

18. Click Start, All Programs, Microsoft Exchange Server 2007, and then click Exchange Management Console. Click OK to close the dialog box stating that you have unlicensed servers.

19. Highlight Server Configuration in the console tree pane and view StudentXX-B in the detail pane. The Role column lists the roles that were successfully installed.

20. Close the Exchange Management Console.

21. Click Start, All Programs, Microsoft Exchange Server 2007, and then click Exchange Management Shell. The Exchange Management Shell window appears.

22. At the command prompt, type **get-ExchangeServer | Format-List** and press Enter to view the installed server roles on StudentXX-A and StudentXX-B.

23. Type **Get-SetupLog %systemroot%\ExchangeSetupLogs\ExchangeSetup.log–error–tree** and press Enter. Once the log file has been parsed, view the results.

24. Type **Get-SetupLog %systemroot%\ExchangeSetupLogs\ExchangeSetup.msilog–error–tree** and press Enter. Once the log file has been parsed, view the results.

25. Close the Exchange Management Shell.

26. Click Start and click My Computer. Navigate to the root of the Exchange Server 2007 media and double click the **setup.exe** file. After a few moments, the Exchange Server 2007 welcome screen appears.

27. Click **Step 5: Get Critical Updates for Microsoft Exchange**. Internet Explorer opens and directs you to the Microsoft Update Web site. Follow the instructions on the Web site to scan for and apply any critical updates that are required by your version of Exchange Server 2007.

28. Close all windows on your desktop.

Exercise 3.3	Deploying the Third Exchange Server
Overview	In the following exercise, you will install Exchange Server 2007 SP1 Enteprise Edition on StudentXX-C with the Edge role as depicted earlier in Figure 3-1.
	To complete this lab exercise, StudentXX-C must be started and have network access.
Completion time	40 minutes

1. On StudentXX-C, log in as the local Administrator account.

2. Obtain and install the PowerShell 1.0, .NET Framework 2.0, .NET Framework 2.0 SP1, MMC Version 3.0, and ADAM packages for your platform. You can download these packages for your platform from http://www.microsoft.com/downloads/.

Question 6	*Why does the Edge role require the installation of ADAM?*

3. Press Next to install the components. Insert your Windows Server 2003 installation media when prompted and press OK. After the installation has finished, click Finish and close the Add or Remove Programs window.

4. Click Start and click My Computer. Navigate to the root of the Exchange Server 2007 media and double click the **setup.exe** file.

5. At the Exchange Server 2007 welcome screen, click **Step 4: Install Microsoft Exchange Server 2007 SP1**.

6. At the Exchange Server 2007 SP1 Setup wizard, click Next.

7. At the License Agreement page, select **I accept the terms in the license agreement** and click Next.

8. At the Error Reporting page, ensure that No is selected and click Next.

9. At the Installation Type page, select Custom Exchange Server Installation and click Next.

10. At the Server Role Selection page, select **Edge Role** and **Management Tools**. Click Next.

11. Review the Readiness Checks page for any errors or warnings. If you have not met the proper software, hardware, and AD requirements, the Readiness Checks page will display errors that describe the component that must be installed or the action that must be taken before you are allowed to continue the Exchange Server 2007 installation. You must then install these components or perform the necessary actions and click Retry to perform the readiness checks again.

12. Click the Install button to begin the Exchange Server 2007 installation. At the end of the Exchange Server 2007 installation, deselect **Finalize installation using the Exchange Management Console** and click Finish. Click OK to close the information window and reboot StudentXX-C.

13. After StudentXX-C has rebooted, log in as Administrator.

14. Click Start, All Programs, Microsoft Exchange Server 2007, and then click Exchange Management Console. Click OK to close the dialog box stating that you have unlicensed servers. Notice that you see the Edge Transport and Toolbox nodes in the console tree pane. Highlight Edge Transport in the console tree pane and view StudentXX-C in the detail pane. The Role column indicates that the Edge Transport role was successfully installed.

15. Close the Exchange Management Console.

16. Click Start, All Programs, Microsoft Exchange Server 2007, and then click Exchange Management Shell. The Exchange Management Shell window appears.

17. At the command prompt, type **get-ExchangeServer | Format-List** and press Enter to view the installed server roles on StudentXX-C.

18. Type **Get-SetupLog %systemroot%\ExchangeSetupLogs\ExchangeSetup.log–error–tree** and press Enter. Once the log file has been parsed, view the results.

19. Type **Get-SetupLog %systemroot%\ExchangeSetupLogs\ExchangeSetup.msilog–error–tree** and press Enter. Once the log file has been parsed, view the results.

20. Close the Exchange Management Shell.

21. Click Start and click My Computer. Navigate to the root of the Exchange Server 2007 media and double click the **setup.exe** file. After a few moments, the Exchange Server 2007 welcome screen appears.

22. Click **Step 5: Get Critical Updates for Microsoft Exchange**. Internet Explorer opens and directs you to the Microsoft Update Web site. Follow the instructions on the Web site to scan for and apply any critical updates that are required by your version of Exchange Server 2007.

23. Close all windows on your desktop.

LAB REVIEW QUESTIONS

Completion time   15 minutes

1. Describe what you learned by completing this lab.

2. Why was it unnecessary to prepare Active Directory during the installation of Exchange Server 2007 on StudentXX-B and StudentXX-C?

3. Briefly outline the additional Windows software components required for the Mailbox, Hub, CAS, UM, and Edge server roles.

Table 3-1
Question 3 Answer

Server Role	Required Software
Mailbox	
Hub Transport (Hub)	
Client Access Server (CAS)	
Unified Messaging (UM)	
Edge Transport (Edge)	

4. What restriction is set when you select the Edge role during Exchange Server 2007 installation?

5. You are required to specify Entourage and Outlook 2003 and earlier MAPI client support after selecting which server role?

LAB CHALLENGE 3.1: PERFORMING AN UNATTENDED EXCHANGE SERVER INSTALLATION

Completion time   35 minutes

You have decided to provide fault tolerance for the UM role within your organization by adding the UM role to StudentXX-B. Add the necessary prerequisite software components for the UM role to StudentXX-B and perform an unattended (nongraphical) installation of the UM role. Following installation, verify that the role was correctly installed.

LAB 4
CONFIGURING EXCHANGE SERVER 2007

This lab contains the following exercises and activities:

Exercise 4.1	Configuring Exchange Administrative Roles
Exercise 4.2	Configuring DNS A and MX Records
Exercise 4.3	Configuring the Hub Role
Exercise 4.4	Configuring the Edge Role
Exercise 4.5	Configuring the Mailbox Role
Exercise 4.6	Configuring the CAS Role
Exercise 4.7	Configuring Send and Receive Connectors
Exercise 4.8	Configuring an Outlook 2007 Account
Exercise 4.9	Configuring an Outlook Express Account
Lab Review Questions	
Lab Challenge 4.1	Performing Exchange Server Configuration Using the Exchange Management Shell

BEFORE YOU BEGIN

Lab 4 assumes that setup has been completed as specified in the setup document and that StudentXX-A, StudentXX-B, and StudentXX-C have connectivity to the classroom network and the Internet. Moreover, Lab 4 assumes that you have completed the exercises in previous labs.

> **NOTE**
> *In this lab, you will see the characters XX. When you see these characters, substitute the two-digit number assigned to your computer.*

SCENARIO

After deploying Exchange Server 2007 within your organization on StudentXX-A, StudentXX-B, and StudentXX-C, you must configure the Mailbox, CAS, Hub, and Edge roles on each computer.

In the Lab Challenge, you perform server role configuration using cmdlets within the Exchange Management Shell.

After completing this lab, you will be able to:

- Configure Exchange administrative roles

- Configure DNS A and MX records to support Exchange Server 2007

- Configure the Hub, Edge, Mailbox, and CAS roles on a new Exchange server

- Configure Send and Receive connectors

- Configure Outlook 2007 and Outlook Express email accounts

- Configure Exchange Server roles using cmdlets within the Exchange Management Shell

Estimated lab time: 150 minutes

Exercise 4.1	Configuring Exchange Administrative Roles
Overview	After deploying your Exchange servers, you need to configure the appropriate access for Exchange server administrators. While you require complete access to all Exchange servers within your organization, Tom Hurt will need to administer public folders on the Exchange servers within the organization and Lois Lipshitz will need to perform Exchange administration and maintenance on StudentXX-B only.
	To complete this lab exercise, StudentXX-A and StudentXX-B must be started and have network access.
Completion time	5 minutes

1. On StudentXX-A, log in as Administrator.

2. Click Start, All Programs, Microsoft Exchange Server 2007, and then click Exchange Management Console.

3. In the console tree pane, highlight Organization Configuration. View the existing Exchange administrative role assignments in the detail pane.

Question 1	*What role is the Administrator user account in the StudentXX.com domain granted?*

4. In the action pane, click Add Exchange Administrator.

5. At the Add Exchange Administrator window, click the Browse button, select **Tom Hurt**, and click OK.

6. Select **Exchange Public Folder Administrator role** and click Add. At the Completion page, click Finish.

7. In the action pane, click Add Exchange Administrator.

8. At the Add Exchange Administrator window, click the Browse button, select **Lois Lipshitz**, and click OK.

9. Select **Exchange Server Administrator role** and click the Add button under the Select the server(s) to which this role has access. Select StudentXX-B and click OK.

10. Click Add. At the Completion page, click Finish.

11. Close the Exchange Management Console.

Exercise 4.2	Configuring DNS A and MX Records
Overview	In this exercise, you will create DNS A and MX records for your Edge role server such that Internet email can be relayed to your organization.
	To complete this lab exercise, StudentXX-A must be started and have network access.
Completion time	5 minutes

1. On StudentXX-A, log in as Administrator.

2. Click Start, Administrative Tools, and then click DNS.

3. At the DNS console window, expand the Forward Lookup Zones folder under StudentXX-A in the left pane.

4. Right click StudentXX.com and select New Host (A) from the menu.

5. At the New Host window, type **mail** in the Name dialog box, type the IP address of StudentXX-C in the IP address dialog box, and click Add Host. Click OK to close the confirmation window and click Done to close the New Host window.

6. Right click the zone for your domain and select New Mail Exchanger (MX) from the menu.

7. At the New Resource Record window, type **mail.StudentXX.com** in the Fully qualified domain name (FQDN) of the mail server dialog box and click OK to create the MX record.

Question 2	Why did you not need to specify any information in the Host or child domain dialog box when creating the MX record?

Question 3	What is the use of the Mail server priority number?

8. Close the DNS console.

Exercise 4.3   Configuring the Hub Role

| Overview | Users involved in research and development within the Research department of your organization will be configured with email addresses that have a domain suffix of research.StudentXX.com whereas other users will use email addresses that use the default domain suffix of StudentXX.com. To allow email relay to the users in the Research department, you must configure an accepted domain for research.StudentXX.com on your Hub role servers.

In addition, for the first few months after Exchange Server 2007 deployment, you want to be notified when there is an email relay problem on your Hub role servers so that you can modify your server and network configuration appropriately. As a result, you will set the postmaster email address to Administrator@StudentXX.com.

To complete this lab exercise, StudentXX-A and StudentXX-B must be started and have network access. |
|---|---|
| Completion time | 10 minutes |

1. On StudentXX-A, log in as Administrator.

2. Click Start, All Programs, Microsoft Exchange Server 2007, and then click Exchange Management Console.

3. In the console tree pane of the Exchange Management Console, expand Organization Configuration and highlight Hub Transport.

4. In the result pane, click the Accepted Domains tab.

Question 4	*What is the default accepted domain and why?*

5. In the action pane, click New Accepted Domain.

6. At the New Accepted Domain window, type **Research Department Domain** in the Name dialog box. Next, type **research.StudentXX.com** in the Accepted Domain dialog box.

7. Ensure that Authoritative Domain is selected and click New.

8. At the Completion page, click Finish and close the Exchange Management Console.

9. Click Start, All Programs, Microsoft Exchange Server 2007, and then click Exchange Management Shell.

10. Type **Get-TransportServer | Format-List Name,ExternalPostMasterAddress** and press Enter.

Question 5	*Is there a postmaster account configured by default?*

11. Type **Set-TransportServer –Identity StudentXX-A –ExternalPostMasterAddress Administrator@StudentXX.com** and press Enter.

12. Type **Set-TransportServer –Identity StudentXX-B –ExternalPostMasterAddress Administrator@StudentXX.com** and press Enter.

13. Type **Get-TransportServer | Format-List Name,ExternalPostMasterAddress** and press Enter. Verify that the postmaster for your Hub role servers (StudentXX-A and StudentXX-B) is Administrator@StudentXX.com.

14. Close the Exchange Management Shell.

Exercise 4.4	Configuring the Edge Role
Overview	Before your organization can use the Edge role to relay external email, you must create an Edge subscription file on StudentXX-C and import it on a Hub role server within the HeadOffice site (either StudentXX-A or StudentXX-B).
	To complete this lab exercise, StudentXX-A, Student-XX-B, and StudentXX-C must be started and have network access.
Completion time	15 minutes

1. On StudentXX-C, log in as the local Administrator account.

2. Click Start, All Programs, Microsoft Exchange Server 2007, and then click Exchange Management Shell.

3. At the Exchange Management Shell prompt, type **New-EdgeSubscription –file "C:\EdgeSubscriptionExport.xml"** and press Enter.

4. When prompted to confirm the action, type **y** and press Enter.

5. Close the Exchange Management Shell.

6. Copy the C:\EdgeSubscriptionExport.xml file to removable media such as a memory stick or portable hard drive.

Question 6	*Within what time period must you import the Edge subscription file on a Hub role server?*

7. On StudentXX-A, log in as Administrator.

8. Click Start, All Programs, Microsoft Exchange Server 2007, and then click Exchange Management Console.

9. In the console tree pane of the Exchange Management Console, expand Organization Configuration and highlight Hub Transport.

10. In the result pane, click the Edge Subscriptions tab.

Question 7	*Are there any Edge subscriptions configured by default?*

11. In the action pane, click New Edge Subscription.

12. At the New Edge Subscription window, select **HeadOffice** in the Active Directory site drop-down box.

13. Next, click Browse, navigate to and select the EdgeSubscriptionExport.xml file that you created on the Edge role server, and click OK.

14. Click New. The Completion page appears.

15. Click Finish to close the New Edge Subscription window. The Edge subscription should appear under the Edge Subscriptions tab in the result pane.

16. Close the Exchange Management Console.

17. Click Start, All Programs, Microsoft Exchange Server 2007, and then click Exchange Management Shell.

18. At the Exchange Management Shell prompt, type **Start-EdgeSynchronization** and press Enter. Examine the output for errors.

19. Close the Exchange Management Shell.

Exercise 4.5 Configuring the Mailbox Role

| Overview | As part of your Mailbox role configuration, you wish to move the location of the default storage groups, mailbox databases, and public folder databases on StudentXX-A and StudentXX-B. Although you would normally move these to another hard disk or RAID array in a production environment, you will move them to directories under the root of C:\ on each Mailbox role server. In addition, you will create additional storage groups and mailbox databases as well as set storage limits on the mailbox and public folder databases on StudentXX-A and StudentXX-B.

To complete this lab exercise, StudentXX-A and Student-XX-B must be started and have network access. |
|---|---|
| Completion time | 40 minutes |

1. On StudentXX-A, log in as Administrator. Create the C:\SG1, C:\SG2, and C:\SG3 folders.

2. On StudentXX-B, log in as Administrator. Create the C:\SG1, C:\SG2, and C:\SG3 folders.

3. On StudentXX-A, log in as Administrator.

4. Click Start, All Programs, Microsoft Exchange Server 2007, and then click Exchange Management Console. The Exchange Management Console window appears.

5. In the console tree pane, expand Server Configuration and highlight Mailbox.

6. In the detail pane, highlight StudentXX-A. View the storage groups in the work pane. Expand them to view the databases within.

7. In the detail pane, highlight StudentXX-B. View the storage groups in the work pane. Expand them to view the databases within. If StudentXX-B does not have a Second Storage Group that contains a Public Folder database, you will create them later in this exercise.

Question 8	What storage groups and databases are configured by default on StudentXX-A and StudentXX-B?

8. In the detail pane, highlight StudentXX-A and select the First Storage Group in the work pane.

9. In the action pane, click Move Storage Group Path.

10. At the Move Storage Group Path window, click Browse beside the Log files path dialog box, select **C:\SG1**, and click OK.

11. Beside the System files path dialog box, click Browse, select **C:\SG1**, and click OK.

12. Click Move. When prompted to confirm that databases within the storage group will be unavailable during the move operation, click Yes.

13. Click Finish at the Completion page to close the Move Storage Group Path window.

14. In the work pane, highlight Second Storage Group.

15. In the action pane, click Move Storage Group Path.

16. At the Move Storage Group Path window, click Browse beside the Log files path dialog box, select **C:\SG2**, and click OK.

17. Beside the System files path dialog box, click Browse, select **C:\SG2**, and click OK.

18. Click Move. When prompted to confirm that databases within the storage group will be unavailable during the move operation, click Yes. The Completion page appears.

19. Click Finish at the Completion page to close the Move Storage Group Path window.

20. In the work pane, highlight Mailbox Database under the First Storage Group.

21. In the action pane, click Move Database Path.

22. At the Move Database Path window, click Browse beside the Database file path dialog box, select **C:\SG1**, and click Save.

23. Click Move. When prompted to confirm that the database will be unavailable during the move operation, click Yes.

24. Click Finish at the Completion page to close the Move Database Path window.

25. In the work pane, highlight Public Folder Database.

26. In the action pane, click Move Database Path.

27. At the Move Database Path window, click Browse beside the Database file path dialog box, select **C:\SG2**, and click Save.

28. Click Move. When prompted to confirm that the database will be unavailable during the move operation, click Yes.

29. Click Finish at the Completion page to close the Move Database Path window.

30. Highlight StudentXX-B in the detail pane. Using the same procedure outlined in Steps 8 to 29, move the default storage groups and databases to C:\SG1 and C:\SG2 on

StudentXX-B. If StudentXX-B does not have a Second Storage Group that contains a Public Folder database, you will create them later in this exercise.

31. When finished, highlight StudentXX-A in the detail pane.

32. In the action pane, click New Storage Group.

33.. At the New Storage Group window, type **Third Storage Group** in the Storage group name field.

34. Beside the Log files path dialog box, click Browse, select **C:\SG3**, and click OK.

35. Beside the System files path dialog box, click Browse, select **C:\SG3**, and click OK.

36. Click New. Click Finish at the Completion page to close the New Storage Group window.

37. In the work pane, highlight Third Storage Group and click New Mailbox Database in the action pane.

38. At the New Mailbox Database window, type **Second Mailbox Database** in the Mailbox database name field. Beside the Database file path dialog box, click Browse, select **C:\SG3**, and click OK.

39. Verify that Mount this database is selected to ensure that the database will be available for use after creation and click New.

40. Click Finish at the Completion page to close the New Mailbox Database window.

41. Close the Exchange Management Console.

42. Highlight StudentXX-B in the detail pane. Using the same procedure outlined in Steps 32 to 41, create a new storage group called **Third Storage Group** as well as a mailbox database called **Second Mailbox Database**. All storage group and database files should reside in **C:\SG3** on StudentXX-B. If StudentXX-B does not have a Second Storage Group that contains a Public Folder database, create it using the same process outlined in Steps 32 to 41 (select New Public Folder Database instead of New Mailbox Database). The Second Storage Group and Public Folder database should store files in the C:\SG2 directory on StudentXX-B.

43. When finished, highlight StudentXX-A in the detail pane.

44. In the work pane, highlight the Mailbox Database under the First Storage Group and click Properties in the action pane.

45. Highlight the Limits tab and configure the following limits:

   - Issue warning at 409600 KB (400 MB)

   - Prohibit send at 460800 KB (450 MB)

- Prohibit send and receive at 512000 KB (500 MB)

- Warning message interval: Run daily at 2:00 a.m.

46. Click OK when finished.

47. In the work pane, highlight the Public Folder Database under the Second Storage Group and click Properties in the action pane.

48. Highlight the Limits tab and configure the following limits:

- Issue warning at 102400 KB (100 MB)

- Prohibit post at 122880 KB (120 MB)

- Maximum item size of 15360 KB (15 MB)

- Warning message interval: Run daily at 2:00 a.m.

49. Highlight StudentXX-B in the detail pane. Using the same procedure outlined in Steps 44 to 48, configure the same storage limits on the Mailbox Database and Public Folder Database on StudentXX-B.

50. Close the Exchange Management Console.

Exercise 4.6	Configuring the CAS Role
Overview	Your organization plans to allow email access to POP3, IMAP4, Outlook Anywhere, and Outlook Web Access (OWA) clients. To ensure security for OWA, file server access will not be allowed for OWA users from a public computer.
	To complete this lab exercise, StudentXX-A and StudentXX-B must be started and have network access.
Completion time	15 minutes

1. On StudentXX-A, log in as Administrator.

2. Click Start, All Programs, Administrative Tools, and then click Services.

3. At the Services console, right click Microsoft Exchange IMAP4 in the right pane and click Properties. Select Automatic in the Startup type drop-down box and click Apply. Next, click Start and click OK.

4. At the Services console, right click Microsoft Exchange POP3 in the right pane and click Properties. Select Automatic in the Startup type drop-down box and click Apply. Next, click Start and click OK.

5. Close the Services console.

6. Click Start, All Programs, Microsoft Exchange Server 2007, and then click Exchange Management Console.

7. In the console tree pane, expand Server Configuration and highlight Client Access.

8. In the action pane, click Enable Outlook Anywhere.

9. At the Enable Outlook Anywhere window, type **StudentXX-A.StudentXX.com** in the External host name field. Select NTLM authentication and click Enable.

10. Click Finish at the Completion screen.

11. In the work pane, highlight owa (Default Web Site) under the Outlook Web Access tab and click Properties in the action pane.

12. Highlight the Remote File Servers tab. Select Allow in the drop-down box and click Configure. In the Internal Domain Suffix List window, type **StudentXX.com** in the dialog box, click Add, and then click OK.

Question 9	What file servers are OWA clients allowed to connect to?

13. Highlight the Private Computer File Access tab and ensure that the following items are selected (enabled):

  - Enable direct file access

  - Enable WebReady Document Viewing

  - Windows File Shares

  - Windows SharePoint Services

14. Highlight the Public Computer File Access tab and ensure that the following items are deselected (disabled):

  - Enable direct file access

  - Enable WebReady Document Viewing

  - Windows File Shares

  - Windows SharePoint Services

Question 10	What must an OWA user select at the OWA logon screen to access file shares?

15. Close the Exchange Management Console.

16. On StudentXX-B, log in as Administrator.

17. Using the same procedure outlined in Steps 2 to 14, configure the POP3 and IMAP4 services to start automatically, enable Outlook Anywhere using an external host name of **StudentXX-B.StudentXX.com**, and configure OWA to allow access to all file servers and features from a private computer only.

Exercise 4.7	Configuring Send and Receive Connectors
Overview	Although the default Send and Receive connectors on your Hub and Edge role servers provide for email relay and connections from POP3 and IMAP4 clients, your organization has some additional connector needs.
	First, the Macintosh IMAP email clients within your organization will be configured to send SMTP email to StudentXX-A using port 1587 and TLS authentication. As a result, you will need to configure a receive connector on StudentXX-A that allows for connections.
	In addition, you wish to ensure that any emails sent to recipients in the hotmail.com, gmail.com, and yahoo.com domains are no larger than 512 KB. To do this, you must create a send connector that applies to your Edge role server that provides the appropriate restrictions.
	To complete this lab exercise, StudentXX-A, StudentXX-B, and StudentXX-C must be started and have network access.
Completion time	10 minutes

1. On StudentXX-A, log in as Administrator.

2. Click Start, All Programs, Microsoft Exchange Server 2007, and then click Exchange Management Console.

3. At the Exchange Management Console window, expand Server Configuration in the console tree, click Hub Transport, and highlight StudentXX-A in the result pane.

> **Question 11**   *What two receive connectors are configured by default on StudentXX-A and what purpose do they serve?*

4. In the action pane, click New Receive Connector.

5. At the New SMTP Receive Connector window, type **Macintosh IMAP Clients** in the Name field, select Custom from the Select the intended use for this Receive connector drop-down box, and click Next.

6. At the Local Network settings page, type **StudentXX-A.StudentXX.com** in the dialog box at the bottom of the screen and click Edit.

7. At the Edit Receive Connector Binding window, type **1587** in the Port dialog box and click OK.

8. Click Next. At the Remote Network settings page, click Next.

9. Review your selections and click New. Click Finish to close the New SMTP Receive Connector window.

10. In the work pane, highlight Macintosh IMAP Clients and click Properties in the action pane.

11. Highlight the Authentication tab and ensure that Transport Layer Security (TLS) is selected. Next, highlight the Permission Groups tab and ensure that Exchange users is selected. Click OK when finished.

12. Expand Organization Configuration in the console tree, highlight Hub Transport, and click the Send Connectors tab in the result pane.

13. In the action pane, click New Send Connector.

14. At the New SMTP Send Connector window, type **Hotmail, Gmail, and Yahoo Mail** in the Name field. In the Select the intended use for this Send connector drop-down box, ensure that Internet is selected and click Next.

15. At the Address space page, click Add, type **hotmail.com** in the Address dialog box, select Include all subdomains, and click OK.

16. Click Add again, type **gmail.com** in the Address dialog box, type **2** in the Cost dialog box, select Include all subdomains, and click OK.

17. Click Add again, type **yahoo.com** in the Address dialog box, type **3** in the Cost dialog box, select Include all subdomains, and click OK.

18. Click Next. At the Network settings page, click Next.

19. At the Source Server page, click X to remove any existing servers. Next, click Add, select your StudentXX-C edge subscription, and click OK.

20. When finished, click Next. Review your selections and click New.

21. Click Finish to close the New SMTP Send Connector window.

22. Highlight the Hotmail, Gmail, and Yahoo Mail send connector under the Send Connectors tab in the detail pane and click Properties in the action pane.

23. On the General tab of send connector properties, type **512** in the Maximum message size (KB) dialog box and click OK.

24. Close the Exchange Management Console.

Exercise 4.8   Configuring an Outlook 2007 Account

Overview	To test various Exchange Server 2007 functionalities in this lab manual, you will need to set up a MAPI account within Outlook 2007. In this lab exercise, you will install Outlook 2007 on StudentXX-A and configure an Exchange (MAPI) email account for yourself (Administrator).
	To complete this lab exercise, StudentXX-A must be started and have network access. In addition, you must have Office 2007 installation media.
Completion time	20 minutes

1. On StudentXX-A, log in as Administrator.

2. Install Office 2007 with the Outlook 2007 components at minimum.

3. Click Start, All Programs, Microsoft Office, and then click Microsoft Office Outlook 2007. If the Office 2007 Startup wizard appears, click Next. Select No and click Next. Select Continue with no e-mail support and click Finish. Close Outlook 2007.

4. Click Start, Control Panel, Mail. At the Mail Setup—Outlook window, click E-mail Accounts. If prompted to enable RSS feeds, click Yes.

5. In the Account Settings window, click New.

6. At the Add New E-mail Account window, select Manually configure server settings or additional server types and click Next.

7. At the Choose E-mail Service page, select Microsoft Exchange and click Next.

8. Type **StudentXX-A.StudentXX.com** in the Microsoft Exchange Server dialog box, deselect **Use Cached Exchange Mode**, type **Administrator** in the User Name dialog box, and click Check Name. After the Exchange server and user names are underlined, click Next.

9. At the Congratulations! screen, click Finish to close the Add New E-mail Account window.

10. Close the Mail Setup—Outlook window.

11. Click Start, All Programs, Microsoft Office, and then click Microsoft Office Outlook 2007. Verify that Outlook 2007 opens without errors and close Outlook 2007.

Exercise 4.9   Configuring an Outlook Express Account

Overview	To test Exchange Server 2007 functionality in this lab manual, you will also need to set up an IMAP4 account within Outlook Express. In this lab exercise, you will configure Outlook Express to obtain email for your user account (Administrator) using IMAP4 and send email using SMTP.
	To complete this lab exercise, StudentXX-A must be started and have network access.
Completion time	5 minutes

1. On StudentXX-A, log in as Administrator.

2. Click Start, All Programs, and then Outlook Express. If you are prompted to make Outlook Express the default mail client on your computer, deselect **Always perform this check when starting Outlook Express** and click No. The Outlook Express window appears.

3. Select the Tools menu, click Accounts.

4. At the Internet Accounts window, click the Add button and select Mail from the side menu.

5. When the Internet Connection Wizard window appears, type **Administrator** in the Display name dialog box and click Next.

6. At the Internet E-mail Address page, type **Administrator@StudentXX.com** in the E-mail address dialog box and click Next.

7. At the E-mail Server Names page, select IMAP from the drop-down box. Next, type **StudentXX-A.StudentXX.com** in both the Incoming mail (POP3, IMAP, HTTP) server dialog box and the Outgoing mail (SMTP) server dialog box. Click Next when finished.

8. At the Internet Mail Logon screen, type **Administrator** in the Account name dialog box and the associated password in the Password dialog box. Select **Require logon using Secure Password Authentication (SPA)** and click Next.

9. Click Finish to close the Internet Connection Wizard window.

10. Highlight your IMAP4 account in the Internet Accounts window and click Properties.

11. Highlight the Advanced tab and select **This server requires a secure connection (SSL) for both Outgoing mail and Incoming mail** and click OK.

12. Close the Internet Accounts window. When prompted to synchronize with the mail server, click Yes.

> NOTE
>
> *You will receive a warning message stating that the certificate on the email server cannot be validated. This certificate will be replaced with a new one that can be validated in Lab 9. Until then, you can safely disregard these warnings.*

13. Close Outlook Express.

LAB REVIEW QUESTIONS

> **Completion time   15 minutes**

1. Describe what you learned by completing this lab.

2. Does it matter what Mail server priority number is chosen in Lab Exercise 4.2? Explain.

3. In Lab Exercise 4.3, explain why you should configure the postmaster account to a different user account (not Administrator@StudentXX.com) after a few months in a production environment.

4. Why was it unnecessary to import the Edge subscription file into StudentXX-B during Lab Exercise 4.4?

5. In Lab Exercise 4.5, you configured your storage groups and databases to reside on C:\. Explain why this is poor practice in a production environment.

6. Why should you restrict access to file shares and documents for OWA users?

7. Why are the POP3 and IMAP4 services disabled by default?

8. Why did you need to configure the connector for StudentXX-C on the StudentXX-A computer?

LAB CHALLENGE 4.1: PERFORMING EXCHANGE SERVER CONFIGURATION USING THE EXCHANGE MANAGEMENT SHELL

> **Completion time   25 minutes**

Although you have configured StudentXX-A, StudentXX-B, and StudentXX-C using the Exchange Management Console in Lab Exercise 4.1 and 4.3 through 4.7, you can also perform Exchange server configuration using cmdlets within the Exchange Management Shell.

Use the Exchange Management Shell to perform the following additional configuration tasks on your Exchange servers:

*   Configure Celine DeVries as an Exchange View-Only Administrator.

*   Ensure that email sent to recipients with a domain suffix of marketing. StudentXX.com will be processed by your Hub role servers and sent to the appropriate mailboxes in StudentXX.com.

*   Create a new storage group called Fourth Storage Group on StudentXX-B that contains a mailbox database called Third Mailbox Database. All files for the storage group and database should reside in the C:\SG4 folder.

- Set the following limits on the Third Mailbox Database:

  o Issue warning at 409600 KB (400 MB)

  o Prohibit send at 460800 KB (450 MB)

  o Prohibit send and receive at 512000 KB (500 MB)

- Ensure that any outgoing Internet email to recipients in the rocketmail.com domain are limited to 1 MB in size.

LAB 5
CONFIGURING RECIPIENT OBJECTS

This lab contains the following exercises and activities:

Exercise 5.1	Configuring Mailbox Users
Exercise 5.2	Providing Unique Mailbox User Configuration
Exercise 5.3	Configuring Mailbox User Permissions
Exercise 5.4	Configuring Mail Users
Exercise 5.5	Configuring Mail Contacts
Exercise 5.6	Configuring Mail-Enabled Groups
Exercise 5.7	Configuring Resource Mailboxes
Exercise 5.8	Moving Mailboxes
Exercise 5.9	Disabling and Reconnecting a Mailbox
Lab Review Questions	
Lab Challenge 5.1	Configuring Recipients Using the Exchange Management Shell
Lab Challenge 5.2	Creating a Linked Mailbox User

BEFORE YOU BEGIN

Lab 5 assumes that setup has been completed as specified in the setup document and that StudentXX-A, StudentXX-B, and StudentXX-C have connectivity to the classroom network and the Internet. Moreover, Lab 5 assumes that you have completed the exercises in previous labs.

> **NOTE** *In this lab, you will see the characters XX. When you see these characters, substitute the two-digit number assigned to your computer.*

SCENARIO

Now that you have configured the necessary server roles on the Exchange servers within your organization, you can create recipient objects to represent the users within your organization. In this lab, you will create and configure mailbox users, mail users, mail contacts, mail-enabled groups, and resource mailboxes. In addition, you will configure mailbox permissions, move mailboxes, and disable and reconnect a mailbox.

In the Lab Challenge, you will perform recipient object configuration using cmdlets within the Exchange Management Shell, as well as configure linked mailbox users in another forest.

After completing this lab, you will be able to:

- Create and configure mailbox users
- Configure mailbox user permissions
- Create and configure mail users
- Create and configure mail contacts
- Create and configure mail-enabled universal distribution groups
- Create and configure mail-enabled dynamic distribution groups
- Create and configure resource mailboxes
- Move mailboxes
- Disconnect and reconnect mailboxes
- Configure recipient objects using cmdlets within the Exchange Management Shell
- Configure linked mailbox users in an Exchange resource forest

Estimated lab time: 210 minutes

Exercise 5.1	Configuring Mailbox Users
Overview	In this Lab Exercise, you will configure mailboxes for the Active Directory users that you created in Lab 2. In addition, you will set common configuration parameters including protocol support, messaging restrictions, and current project (using a custom attribute). To complete this lab exercise, StudentXX-A and StudentXX-B must be started and have network access.
Completion time	40 minutes

1. On StudentXX-A, log in as Administrator.

2. Click Start, All Programs, Microsoft Exchange Server 2007, and then click Exchange Management Console.

3. In the console tree pane, expand Recipient Configuration and highlight Mailbox.

4. In the action pane, click New Mailbox.

5. At the New Mailbox window, select User Mailbox and click Next.

6. Select Existing users, click the Add button, select Sophia Boren, and click OK.

7. At the Mailbox Settings page, ensure that sophia.boren is listed in the Alias dialog box.

Question 1	*What internal email address will be used for Sophia Boren by default?*

8. Click Browse next to the Mailbox database dialog box, select the Mailbox Database in the First Storage Group on StudentXX-A and click OK.

9. Click Next. Review the summary of your settings and click New.

10. Click Finish to close the New Mailbox window.

11. Highlight Sophia Boren in the detail pane and select Properties from the action pane.

12. On the General tab of user properties, click Custom Attributes, type **Project58** in the Custom attribute 1 dialog box and click OK.

13. Select the Mailbox Features tab, highlight POP3, and click Disable. Next, highlight IMAP4 and click Disable.

14. Select the Mail Flow Settings tab, highlight Delivery Options, and click Properties. Select Maximum recipients, enter 100 in the associated dialog box, and click OK.

15. Highlight Message Size Restrictions and click Properties. Under the Sending message size section, Select Maximum message size (in KB) and enter 10240 in the associated dialog box. Under the Receiving message size section, Select Maximum message size (in KB) and enter 20480 in the associated dialog box. Click OK.

16. Click OK to close mailbox user properties.

17. Using the same procedure outlined in Steps 4 to 16, configure the other mailbox users listed in Table 5-1 with the appropriate settings.

Table 5-1
Mailbox User Configuration Information

User Name	Custom Attribute 1	Enabled Protocols	Maximum Recipients	Maximum Send Message Size	Maximum Receive Message Size
Sophia Boren	Project58	OWA, ActiveSync, MAPI	100	10240	20480
Mel Booker	Project45	OWA, ActiveSync, MAPI, POP3	50	20480	20480
Celine DeVries	Project58	OWA, ActiveSync, MAPI, IMAP4	100	10240	20480
Mark Daly	Project58	OWA, MAPI	100	10240	20480
Tiger Smith	Project45	OWA, ActiveSync, MAPI, IMAP4	50	20480	20480
Meg Roombas	Project58	OWA, ActiveSync, MAPI, IMAP4	100	10240	20480
Jacques Guillere	Project45	OWA, MAPI, POP3	50	20480	20480
Juan Ton	Project45	OWA, ActiveSync, MAPI	50	20480	20480
Sarah Parkers	Project45	OWA, ActiveSync, MAPI, POP3	50	20480	20480
Lois Lipshitz	Project45	OWA, ActiveSync, MAPI, IMAP4	50	20480	20480
Jessica Augustus	Project58	OWA, ActiveSync, MAPI, POP3	100	10240	20480
Tom Hurt	Project58	OWA, ActiveSync, MAPI	100	10240	20480

Table 5-1 (*continued*)

Bernadette Jones	Project58	OWA, MAPI	100	10240	20480
Jennifer Coupland	Project45	OWA, ActiveSync, MAPI	50	20480	20480
Lisa Lackner	Project45	OWA, ActiveSync, MAPI	50	20480	20480
Mathew Kropf	Project45	OWA, ActiveSync, MAPI, IMAP4	50	20480	20480
Matt Adams	Project58	OWA, ActiveSync, MAPI	100	10240	20480
David Schwan	Project58	OWA, MAPI	100	10240	20480

18. Close the Exchange Management Console.

Exercise 5.2	Providing Unique Mailbox User Configuration
Overview	Over time, you will need to provide custom configuration for individual mailbox users to match the needs of the user and organization. In this Lab Exercise, you will provide unique configuration for three mailbox users.
	Mel Booker is the Human Resources Manager and should receive any email sent to HR@StudentXX.com. In addition, Mel Booker accesses his email from a portable wireless device using POP3 that requires plain text formatted email.
	Tom Hurt manages the Production department. While Tom is away on vacation, his supervisor Jennifer Coupland will be performing his duties. As a result, you must ensure that copies of any emails sent to Tom Hurt will be forwarded to Jennifer Coupland.
	David Schwan sends emails to the other production team on a regular basis but often sends emails to Matt Adams in the Sales department instead of Matthew Kropf in the Production department. To prevent this, you will configure Matt Adams' mailbox to reject email from David Schwan.
	To complete this lab exercise, StudentXX-A and StudentXX-B must be started and have network access.
Completion time	10 minutes

1. On StudentXX-A, log in as Administrator.

2. Click Start, All Programs, Microsoft Exchange Server 2007, and then click Exchange Management Console.

3. In the console tree pane, expand Recipient Configuration and highlight Mailbox.

4. Highlight Mel Booker in the detail pane and select Properties from the action pane.

5. Click the E-Mail Addresses tab and deselect **Automatically update e-mail addresses based on e-mail address policy**. Click Add and type **HR@StudentXX.com** in the E-mail address dialog box of the SMTP Address window and click OK.

6. Click the Mailbox Features tab, highlight POP3, and select Properties. Deselect **Use protocol default**, select Text from the drop-down box, and click OK.

7. Click OK to close mailbox user properties.

8. Highlight Tom Hurt in the detail pane and select Properties from the action pane.

9. Click the Mail Flow Settings tab, highlight Delivery Options, and click Properties. Select **Forward to**, click Browse, highlight Jennifer Coupland, and click OK. Select **Deliver message to both forwarding address and mailbox** and click OK.

10. Click OK to close mailbox user properties.

11. Highlight Matt Adams in the detail pane and select Properties from the action pane.

12. Click the Mail Flow Settings tab, highlight Message Delivery Restrictions, and click Properties. Under the **Reject messages from** section, click **Senders in the following list** and click Add. Select David Schwan and click OK. Click OK to return to mailbox user properties.

13. Click OK to close mailbox user properties.

14. Close the Exchange Management Console.

Exercise 5.3	Configuring Mailbox User Permissions
Overview	Understanding when to configure and use Send as, Send on behalf, and Full access permissions with mailbox users is vital for any Exchange administrator. In this Lab Exercise, you will configure the different mailbox permissions on the Tiger Smith mailbox user and test your permissions assignments afterwards. To complete this lab exercise, StudentXX-A and StudentXX-B must be started and have network access.
Completion time	15 minutes

1. On StudentXX-A, log in as Administrator.

2. Click Start, All Programs, Microsoft Exchange Server 2007, and then click Exchange Management Console.

3. In the console tree pane, expand Recipient Configuration and highlight Mailbox.

4. In the result pane, highlight Tiger Smith and click Properties from the action pane.

5. Click the Mail Flow Settings tab, highlight Delivery Options, and click Properties. Under the Send on behalf section, click Add, highlight Administrator, and click OK. Click OK to return to mailbox user properties.

6. Click OK to close mailbox user properties.

Question 2	*What does Send on behalf permission allow Administrator to do as Tiger Smith?*

7. In the result pane, highlight Tiger Smith and click Manage Send As Permission in the action pane.

8. At the Manage Send As Permission window, click Add, select Administrator, and click OK. Click Manage.

9. Click Finish to close the Manage Send As Permission window.

Question 3	*What does Send as permission allow Administrator to do as Tiger Smith?*

10. In the result pane, highlight Tiger Smith and click Manage Full Access Permission in the action pane.

11. At the Manage Full Access Permission window, click Add, select Administrator, and click OK. Click Manage.

12. Click Finish to close the Manage Full Access Permission window.

Question 4	*What does Full access permission allow Administrator to do as Tiger Smith?*

13. Close the Exchange Management Console.

14. Click Start, All Programs, Microsoft Office, and then click Microsoft Office Outlook 2007.

15. Click the Tools menu and select Account Settings.

16. Highlight Administrator@StudentXX.com under the E-mail tab and click Change.

17. At the Change E-mail Account window, click More Settings.

18. At the Microsoft Exchange window, highlight the Advanced tab and click the Add button. Type **Tiger Smith** and click OK.

Question 5	*Why are you allowed to add Tiger Smith's mailbox to Administrator's Outlook account settings?*

19. Click OK to return to the Change E-mail Account window and click Next. Click Finish to close the Change E-mail Account window and click Close to close the Account Settings window.

20. In the left pane of Outlook 2007, expand Mailbox—Tiger Smith and highlight Inbox.

21. Click New to compose a new email. At the new message window, click the Options tab and click Fields and then click Show From.

22. Click the From button and select Tiger Smith. Next, click the To button and select Administrator.

23. Type **Permissions Test** in the Subject field and click the Send button.

24. Expand Mailbox—Administrator in the left pane of Outlook 2007 and highlight Inbox. Double click the email from Tiger Smith.

Question 6	Who is listed in the From box of the email and why?

25. Close your email and close Outlook 2007.

Exercise 5.4	Configuring Mail Users
Overview	To provide effective marketing for your company's products, you have hired two marketing specialists from a marketing agency: Courtney Davies and Mike Moritz. Courtney and Mike will be working alongside the rest of your Marketing department for the next six months and will require domain access but will not require a mailbox because they already have a mailbox at their home organization. To facilitate Courtney and Mike, you will need to configure mail users for them so that others within the organization can easily locate them within the Global Address List and send email to their external email address.

To complete this lab exercise, StudentXX-A and StudentXX-B must be started and have network access. |
| Completion time | 10 minutes |

1. On StudentXX-A, log in as Administrator.

2. Click Start, All Programs, Microsoft Exchange Server 2007, and then click Exchange Management Console.

3. In the console tree pane, expand Recipient Configuration and highlight Mail Contact.

4. In the action pane, click New Mail User.

5.   At the New Mail User window, select Existing user, click the Browse button, select Courtney Davies in the Select User window that appears and click OK. Click Next.

6.   At the Mail Settings page, ensure that courtney.davies is listed in the Alias dialog box.

Question 7	What internal email address will be used for Courtney Davies by default?

7.   Click Edit next to the External e-mail address dialog box, type **cdavies@marketinghorizons.com** in the SMTP Address window that appears and click OK.

8.   Click Next. Review the summary of your settings and click New.

9.   Click Finish to close the New Mail User window.

10. Highlight Courtney Davies in the detail pane and select Properties from the action pane.

11. On the General tab of mail user properties, click Custom Attributes, type **Project45** in the Custom attribute 1 dialog box and click OK.

12. Select the Mail Flow Settings tab, highlight Message Size Restrictions, and click Properties. Under the Receiving message size section, Select Maximum message size (in KB) and enter **10240** in the associated dialog box. Click OK.

13. Click OK to close mail user properties.

14. Using the same procedure outlined in Steps 4 to 13, configure a mail user for the existing Mike Moritz user account that uses an alias of **mike.moritz** and an external email address of **mikem@gnumarketing.org**. For the Mike Moritz mail user, ensure that Custom attribute 1 is set to Project58 and that the maximum receiving message size is set to 10240 KB.

15. Close the Exchange Management Console.

Exercise 5.5	Configuring Mail Contacts
Overview	Your organization employs two contract janitorial workers. Joe Mos is the daytime janitorial worker and Judy Chong is the nighttime janitorial worker. Since Joe and Judy have existing email accounts on an external email system and do not need domain access, you will create mail contacts for them to ensure that users within your organization can send special cleanup requests as necessary. Since these requests will be simple, you wish to ensure that they are not sent in MAPI rich text and are less than 1024 KB (1 MB).
	To complete this lab exercise, StudentXX-A and StudentXX-B must be started and have network access.
Completion time	10 minutes

1. On StudentXX-A, log in as Administrator.

2. Click Start, All Programs, Microsoft Exchange Server 2007, and then click Exchange Management Console.

3. In the console tree pane, expand Recipient Configuration and highlight Mail Contact.

4. In the action pane, click New Mail Contact.

5. At the New Mail Contact window, ensure that New contact is selected and click Next.

6. At the Contact Information page, click Browse, select the Production OU, and click OK.

7. Type **Joe** in the First name dialog box, type **Mos** in the Last name dialog box and type **joe.mos** in the Alias dialog box.

8. Click Edit next to the External e-mail address dialog box, type **joemos@cleanupsolutions.com** in the SMTP Address window and click OK.

9. Click Next. Review the summary of your settings and click New.

10. Click Finish to close the New Mail Contact window.

11. Select the Joe Mos mail contact in the detail pane and click Properties in the action pane.

12. In the Use MAPI rich text format window, select Never from the drop-down box.

13. Select the Mail Flow Settings tab, highlight Message Size Restrictions, and click Properties. Under the Receiving message size section, select Maximum message size (in KB) and enter **1024** in the associated dialog box. Click OK.

14. Click OK to close mail contact properties.

15. Using the same procedure outlined in Steps 4 to 15, configure a mail contact for Judy Chong in the Production OU that uses an alias of **judy.chong** and an external email address of **judyc@tps.org**. For the Judy Chong mail contact, ensure that MAPI rich text format is disabled, and that the maximum receiving message size is set to 1024 KB.

16. Close the Exchange Management Console.

Exercise 5.6   Configuring Mail-Enabled Groups

Overview

Certain messages within your organization must be relayed to all project managers or project members. As a result, you plan to implement mail-enabled groups to simplify sending email to multiple recipients.

Because there are only three project managers and these project managers often require special permissions on resources, you plan to create a mail-enabled universal security group with the email alias Project-Managers@StudentXX.com. For project members, you plan to create two dynamic distribution groups that search for the appropriate custom attribute within the recipient objects in your domain. Users should be able to email Project45@StudentXX.com and Project58@StudentXX.com to relay email to the appropriate project members.

To complete this lab exercise, StudentXX-A and StudentXX-B must be started and have network access.

Completion time	15 minutes

1. Click Start, All Programs, Microsoft Exchange Server 2007, and then click Exchange Management Console.

2. In the console tree pane, expand Recipient Configuration and highlight Distribution Group.

3. In the action pane, click New Distribution Group.

4. At the New Distribution Group window, ensure that New group is selected and click Next.

5. At the Group Information page, select Security in the Group type section. Next, click Browse, select the StudentXX.com domain, and click OK. Type **Project-Managers** in the Name dialog box and note that the preWindows 2000 name and alias are given the same value.

6. Click Next. Review the summary of your settings and click New.

7. Click Finish to close the New Distribution Group window.

8. Select the Project-Managers group in the detail pane and click Properties in the action pane.

9. Highlight the Members tab and click Add. Hold down the Ctrl key on your keyboard; select Sophia Boren, Tiger Smith, and Tom Hurt; and click OK.

10. Click OK again to close the properties of the mail-enabled universal security group.

11. In the action pane, click New Dynamic Distribution Group.

12. At the New Dynamic Distribution Group window, click Browse, select the StudentXX.com domain, and click OK.

13. Next, type **Project58** in the Name dialog box and note that the same value is automatically placed in the Alias dialog box. Click Next.

14. At the Filter Settings page, click Browse, select StudentXX.com, and click OK.

Question 8	Why did you need to ensure that the Project58 dynamic distribution group searches the entire domain?

15. Click Next. Select **Custom Attribute 1 equals Value** in the **Step 1: Select condition(s)** dialog box. Next, click **specified** in the **Step 2: Edit the condition(s) dialog box**, type **Project58**, click Add, and then click OK.

16. Perform a test search for all recipients within your domain with the first custom attribute set to Project58 by clicking Preview. Click OK when finished and click Next.

17. Review the summary of your settings and click New.

18. Click Finish to close the New Dynamic Distribution Group window.

19. Using the same procedure outlined in Steps 11 to 18, create another dynamic distribution group called Project45 under StudentXX.com that includes all recipient objects within StudentXX.com with the first custom attribute set to Project45.

20. Close the Exchange Management Console.

21. Click Start, All Programs, Microsoft Office, and then click Microsoft Office Outlook 2007.

22. Click New to compose a new email. In the To dialog box, type **Project-Managers@ StudentXX.com**. Next, type **Project-Managers Group Email Test** in the Subject dialog box and click Send.

23. Click New to compose a new email. In the To dialog box, type **Project45@ StudentXX.com**. Next, type **Project45 Group Email Test** in the Subject dialog box and click Send.

24. Click New to compose a new email. In the To dialog box, type **Project58@ StudentXX.com**. Next, type **Project58 Group Email Test** in the Subject dialog box and click Send.

25. Expand Mailbox—Tiger Smith and highlight Inbox.

Question 9	*What emails did Tiger Smith receive and why?*

26. Close Outlook 2007.

Exercise 5.7   Configuring Resource Mailboxes

Overview	Your organization plans to use the resource scheduling abilities of Outlook to book conference rooms for meetings as well as book the use of a presentation SmartBoard without the use of a delegate to oversee the process. As a result, you must create and configure the appropriate resource mailboxes, enable automatic booking, and configure a book-in policy that does not require a delegate when resource conflicts arise.
	To complete this lab exercise, StudentXX-A and StudentXX-B must be started and have network access.
Completion time	25 minutes

1. On StudentXX-A, log in as Administrator.

2. Click Start, All Programs, Microsoft Exchange Server 2007, and then click Exchange Management Shell.

3. At the Exchange Management Shell prompt, type **Set-ResourceConfig –Resource PropertySchema ('Room/Projector','Room/Whiteboard','Room/WiFi')** and press Enter.

4. Close the Exchange Management Shell.

5. Click Start, All Programs, Microsoft Exchange Server 2007, and then click Exchange Management Console.

6. In the console tree pane, expand Recipient Configuration and highlight Mailbox.

7. In the action pane, click New Mailbox.

8. At the New Mailbox window, select Equipment Mailbox and click Next.

9. At the User Type page, ensure that New user is selected and click Next.

10. Type **SmartBoard** in the Name dialog box, type **SmartBoard** in the User logon name dialog box, and click Next.

11. At the Mailbox Settings page, ensure that the Alias dialog box contains SmartBoard.

12. Click Browse next to the Mailbox database dialog box, select the Mailbox Database in the First Storage Group on StudentXX-A, and click OK.

13. Click Next. Review the summary of your settings and click New.

14. Click Finish to close the New Mailbox window.

15. Highlight SmartBoard in the detail pane and click Properties in the action pane.

16. Select the Resource Information tab, type **1** in the Resource capacity dialog box, and click OK.

17. Click OK to close the properties of the resource mailbox.

18. In the action pane, click New Mailbox.

19. At the New Mailbox window, select Room Mailbox and click Next.

20. At the User Type page, ensure that New user is selected and click Next.

21. Type **ConferenceRoom1** in the Name dialog box, type **ConferenceRoom1** in the User logon name dialog box, and click Next.

22. At the Mailbox Settings page, ensure that the Alias dialog box contains ConferenceRoom1.

23. Click Browse next to the Mailbox database dialog box, select the Mailbox Database in the First Storage Group on StudentXX-A, and click OK.

24. Click Next. Review the summary of your settings and click New.

25. Click Finish to close the New Mailbox window.

26. Highlight ConferenceRoom1 in the detail pane and click Properties in the action pane.

27. Select the Resource Information tab and type **10** in the Resource capacity dialog box. Next, click Add. While holding down the Ctrl key on your keyboard, select Projector and WiFi, and click OK.

28. Click OK to close the properties of the resource mailbox.

29. Using the same procedure outlined in Steps 18 to 28, create and configure the resource mailboxes listed in Table 5-2.

Table 5-2
Resource Mailbox Configuration Information

Resource Mailbox Name	Capacity	Resources
ConferenceRoom1	10	Projector, WiFi
ConferenceRoom2	25	Projector, Whiteboard, WiFi
ConferenceRoom3	10	Projector, Whiteboard
ConferenceRoom4	15	Projector, Whiteboard, WiFi
ConferenceRoom5	18	Whiteboard

30. Close the Exchange Management Console.

31. Click Start, All Programs, Microsoft Exchange Server 2007, and then click Exchange Management Shell.

32. At the Exchange Management Shell prompt, type **Set-MailboxCalendarSettings –Identity 'ConferenceRoom1' –AutomateProcessing:AutoAccept** and press Enter to enable automatic booking on the ConferenceRoom1 resource mailbox.

33. At the Exchange Management Shell prompt, type **Set-MailboxCalendarSettings –Identity 'ConferenceRoom1' –AllBookInPolicy:$true** and press Enter to specify a book-in policy for the ConferenceRoom1 resource mailbox for all users.

34. Using the procedure outlined in the previous two steps, enable automatic booking and specify a book-in policy for all other resource mailboxes.

35. Close the Exchange Management Shell.

36. Click Start, All Programs, Microsoft Office, and then click Microsoft Office Outlook 2007.

37. Under Mailbox—Administrator, highlight Calendar and click New to create a new calendar appointment.

38. Click Invite Attendees. Next, click the To button, select the Project-Managers group, and click Required. Select SmartBoard, click Resources, and click OK.

39. Type **Policies and Procedures Meeting** in the Subject dialog box.

40. Click Rooms next to the Location dialog box, select ConferenceRoom4, click Rooms, and click OK.

41. Select a Start and End time from 3:00 p.m. to 4:00 p.m. tomorrow and click Send.

42. Select tomorrow's date in the Calendar and view your appointment to see if there are any resource conflicts.

43. Close Outlook 2007.

Exercise 5.8	Moving Mailboxes
Overview	All the mailboxes you have created in this lab have been stored within the Mailbox Database on the First Storage Group on StudentXX-A. To provide for fault tolerance, you plan to move mailboxes to other mailbox databases to balance the distribution of mailboxes in your organization. To complete this lab exercise, StudentXX-A and StudentXX-B must be started and have network access.
Completion time	15 minutes

1. On StudentXX-A, log in as Administrator.

2. Click Start, All Programs, Microsoft Exchange Server 2007, and then click Exchange Management Console. The Exchange Management Console window appears.

3. In the console tree pane, expand Recipient Configuration and highlight Mailbox.

4. While holding down the Ctrl key on your keyboard, select Meg Roombas, Jacques Guillere, Juan Ton, Sarah Parkers, Lois Lipshitz, Jessica Augustus, and Tom Hurt in the result pane.

5. Click Move Mailbox in the action pane.

6. At the Move Mailbox window, click Browse, select the Second Mailbox Database in the Third Storage Group on StudentXX-A, and click OK.

7. Click Next. Ensure that Skip the mailbox is selected and click Next.

8. Ensure that Immediately is selected and click Next. Click Move.

9. Once the move operation has completed, click Finish to close the Move Mailbox window.

10. While holding down the Ctrl key on your keyboard, select Bernadette Jones, Jennifer Coupland, Lisa Lackner, Mathew Kropf, Matt Adams, and David Schwan in the result pane.

11. Click Move Mailbox in the action pane.

12. At the Move Mailbox window, click Browse, select the Mailbox Database in the First Storage Group on StudentXX-B, and click OK.

13. Click Next. Ensure that Skip the mailbox is selected and click Next.

14. Ensure that Immediately is selected and click Next. Click Move.

15. Once the move operation has completed, click Finish to close the Move Mailbox window.

16. While holding down the Ctrl key on your keyboard, select SmartBoard, ConferenceRoom1, ConferenceRoom2, ConferenceRoom3, ConferenceRoom4, and ConferenceRoom5 in the result pane.

17. Click Move Mailbox in the action pane.

18. At the Move Mailbox window, click Browse, select the Second Mailbox Database in the Third Storage Group on StudentXX-B, and click OK.

19. Click Next. Ensure that Skip the mailbox is selected and click Next.

20. Ensure that Immediately is selected and click Next. Click Move.

21. Once the move operation has completed, click Finish to close the Move Mailbox window.

22. In the detail pane, click Create Filter.

23. Select Database and Equals from the two drop-down boxes. Click Browse, select the Mailbox Database in the First Storage Group, and click OK.

24. Click Apply Filter in the detail pane.

Question 10	*Who is displayed in the detail pane and why?*

25. Click Remove Filter in the detail pane.

26. Using the procedure outlined in Steps 21 to 25, view the mailboxes in all other mailbox databases to verify that your move operations were successful.

27. Close the Exchange Management Console.

Exercise 5.9	Disabling and Reconnecting a Mailbox
Overview	You have heard that you can disable and reconnect mailboxes when users leave the organization and are replaced by a new hire. As a result, you plan to disable and reconnect the Mark Daly user account to examine the procedure and determine how it can be used within your organization. To complete this lab exercise, StudentXX-A and StudentXX-B must be started and have network access.
Completion time	5 minutes

1. On StudentXX-A, log in as Administrator.

2. Click Start, All Programs, Microsoft Exchange Server 2007, and then click Exchange Management Console. The Exchange Management Console window appears.

3. In the console tree pane, expand Recipient Configuration and highlight Mailbox.

4. In the result pane, select Mark Daly, click Disable in the action pane to remove the Exchange properties from the user and mark the mailbox for deletion. Click Yes to confirm the action.

Question 11	*What would have happened if you chose Delete from the action pane instead of Disable?*

5. In the console tree pane, expand Recipient Configuration and highlight Disconnected Mailbox.

6. In the result pane, select the Mark Daly mailbox and click Connect in the action pane.

7. At the Connect Mailbox window, ensure that User Mailbox is selected and click Next.

8. At the Mailbox Settings page, select Matching user, click Browse, select Mark Daly, and click OK.

9. Ensure that mark.daly is listed in the Alias dialog box and click Next.

10. Click Connect. Click Finish to close the Connect Mailbox window.

11. In the console tree pane, expand Recipient Configuration and highlight Mailbox. Verify that Mark Daly is displayed.

12. Close the Exchange Management Console.

LAB REVIEW QUESTIONS

Completion time	20 minutes

1. Describe what you learned by completing this lab.

2. Give some other examples of when you would need to add an additional email address to a mailbox user.

3. What type of recipient object would you create for newly hired contract employees who *require* domain access but do not require mailboxes because they have active external email accounts?

4. What type of recipient object would you create for newly hired contract employees who *do not require* domain access and do not require mailboxes because they have active external email accounts?

5. Why should you minimize the use of Full access mailbox permission?

6. In an organization, whom do you typically assign the Send on behalf and Send as mailbox permissions to?

7. When would you create a mail-enabled dynamic distribution group instead of a mail-enabled universal group?

8. Explain how resource mailboxes reduce the administrative burden in your organization.

9. Explain why you would move mailboxes between different storage groups on different servers.

10. If a user leaves your organization and their job role is assumed by an existing user, would you disconnect the existing user's mailbox? Explain.

LAB CHALLENGE 5.1: CONFIGURING RECIPIENTS USING THE EXCHANGE MANAGEMENT SHELL

Completion time	25 minutes

Although you have configured recipient objects using the Exchange Management Console in Lab Exercises 5.1 through 5.9, you can also perform recipient configuration using cmdlets within the Exchange Management Shell.

Use the Exchange Management Shell to perform the following additional recipient configuration tasks:

- Create a new mailbox user for John Kerr (alias = john.kerr) in the Marketing OU of StudentXX.com and store the mailbox in the Mailbox Database in the First Storage

Group on StudentXX-A. Also ensure that John has an initial password of Secret123 and that the password must be changed at first logon.

- Ensure that John Kerr has a maximum send size of 5 MB.

- Create a new mail-enabled contact for Julie Bell (alias = julie.bell) in the Production OU of StudentXX.com that has an external email address of bellj@fizzure.net.

- Add Celine DeVries to the Project-Managers mail-enabled universal security group.

- Create a dynamic distribution group under the StudentXX.com domain that includes all mailbox users in the domain that are members of Project58.

- Move Meg Roombas' mailbox to the Mailbox Database in the First Storage Group on StudentXX-A. Ensure that the move operation fails if more than five corrupted messages are found.

LAB CHALLENGE 5.2: CREATING A LINKED MAILBOX USER

Completion time	20 minutes

As the Exchange administrator for your organization, you have been asked to explore the feasibility of deploying an Exchange resource forest. To better understand how master accounts in your forest can interact with linked mailbox users within an Exchange resource forest, you plan to configure a Linked mailbox user for a test user account.

To perform this exercise, you must first have created a cross forest trust relationship in Lab Challenge 2.2 from Lab 2. Next, you must create a user account (First name = Test, Last name = Account, Alias = test.account, Password = Secret123) in the StudentXX.com domain that will serve as the master account. Next, your partner must create a linked mailbox user for your master account in the StudentYY.com domain with the same name and alias. Following this, you can test your linked mailbox user by sending an email to test.account@StudentYY.com and then checking the email using OWA (https://StudentYY-A.StudentYY.com) using the credentials of the master account.

LAB 6
CONFIGURING ADDRESS LISTS, POLICIES, AND BULK MANAGEMENT

This lab contains the following exercises and activities:

Exercise 6.1   Configuring Address Lists

Exercise 6.2   Configuring Email Address Policies

Exercise 6.3   Configuring Messaging Records Management

Exercise 6.4   Configuring Message Journaling

Exercise 6.5   Performing Bulk Management of Recipient Objects

Lab Review Questions

Lab Challenge 6.1   Configuring Address Lists Using the Exchange Management
                        Shell

Lab Challenge 6.2   Creating a PowerShell Script

BEFORE YOU BEGIN

Lab 6 assumes that setup has been completed as specified in the setup document and that StudentXX-A, StudentXX-B, and StudentXX-C have connectivity to the classroom network and the Internet. Moreover, Lab 6 assumes that you have completed the exercises in previous labs.

NOTE	In this lab, you will see the characters XX. When you see these characters, substitute the two-digit number assigned to your computer.

SCENARIO

After configuring recipients within your organization, you plan to configure address lists and Offline Address Books to help MAPI users locate other recipients and configure email address policies to modify the email address structure used by recipient objects. In addition, you plan to implement message compliance using managed folders and journaling to satisfy internal and legal requirements as well as practice bulk management of recipient objects to save future administration.

In the Lab Challenge, you will configure address lists and message compliance using cmdlets within the Exchange Management Shell and configure a PowerShell script that can be used for future administration.

After completing this lab, you will be able to:

- Configure address lists and Offline Address Books

- Configure email address policies

- Configure message compliance using Messaging Records Management (MRM), standard journaling, and premium journaling

- Create and manage recipient objects using bulk management commands within the Exchange Management Shell

- Create PowerShell scripts for bulk management

Estimated lab time: 280 minutes

Exercise 6.1	Configuring Address Lists
Overview	In this Lab Exercise, you will configure address lists for each of your four departments (Accounting, Marketing, Sales, and Production) to help users easily locate recipients by department when composing emails.
	In addition, you will ensure that your new address lists are included in the default Offline Address Book for all users within the organization.
	To complete this lab exercise, StudentXX-A and StudentXX-B must be started and have network access.
Completion time	15 minutes

1. On StudentXX-A, log in as Administrator.

2. Click Start, All Programs, Microsoft Exchange Server 2007, and then click Exchange Management Console.

3. In the console tree pane, expand Organization Configuration and highlight Mailbox.

4. In the action pane, click New Address List.

5. At the New Address List window, type **Marketing Department** in the Name dialog box. Ensure that All recipient types is selected and click Next.

6. At the Conditions page, select **Recipient is in a Department** in the **Step 1: Select Conditions** dialog box, and click **specified** within the **Step 2: Edit the condition(s)** dialog box. Type **Marketing**, click Add, and then click OK.

7. Test your settings by clicking Preview to view the recipient objects with the Marketing department attribute and click OK when finished.

8. Click Next. At the Schedule page, click Next to create the address list immediately.

9. Review the summary of your settings and click New.

10. Click Finish to close the New Address List window.

11. Using the procedure outlined in Steps 4 to 10, create address lists for the Accounting, Sales, and Production departments.

12. In the console tree pane, expand Organization Configuration and highlight Mailbox. Select the Offline Address Book tab in the detail pane, highlight the Default Offline Address Book, and click Properties in the action pane.

13. Highlight the Address Lists tab and select **Include the following address lists**.

14. Click Add, select Marketing Department, and click OK. Repeat this step until all department address lists are added to the Default Offline Address Book.

15. Highlight the Distribution tab. Ensure that Version 2, 3, and 4 clients are supported and that both web-based and public folder distribution methods are selected. Also ensure that web-based distribution is performed using the OAB (Default Web Site) on StudentXX-A and StudentXX-B. When finished, click OK.

16. Click Start, All Programs, Microsoft Office, and then click Microsoft Office Outlook 2007.

17. Click New to compose a new email. Next, click the To button and then click the Address Book drop-down box and select Marketing Department. If you do not see your address lists in the Address Book drop-down box, you may have the **Use Cached Exchange Mode** option set in your Outlook account properties.

Question 1	*What recipient objects are displayed?*

18. Click the Address Book drop-down box and select your other department address lists in turn and examine the list displayed.

19. Press Cancel to return to Outlook 2007 and close all Outlook 2007 windows.

Exercise 6.2   Configuring Email Address Policies

Overview	Your organization has decided to change the email address format used by recipients within your organization. The primary email address used by recipients should now be lastname.firstinitial@StudentXX.com. You must also ensure that external members can still relay email to recipients within your organization using the original email address format alias@StudentXX.com.
	For external contract members (mail-enabled users and mail-enabled contacts), the primary email address should be firstname.lastname-ext@StudentXX.com to identify them as external members.
	To complete this lab exercise, StudentXX-A and StudentXX-B must be started and have network access.
Completion time	15 minutes

1. On StudentXX-A, log in as Administrator.

2. Click Start, All Programs, Microsoft Exchange Server 2007, and then click Exchange Management Console.

3. In the console tree pane, expand Organization Configuration and highlight Hub Transport.

4. Select the E-mail Address Policies tab in the detail pane, highlight Default Policy, and click Edit in the action pane.

5. At the Edit E-mail Address Policy window, click Next. Click Next again.

6. At the E-Mail Addresses page, click Add, select **Last name and first name initial (smithj)**, and click OK.

7. Highlight %s%1g@StudentXX.com and click Set as Reply.

Question 2	*What does Set as Reply do?*

8. Click Next. Click Next again to apply the policy immediately.

9. Click Edit to configure and apply the new policy and click Finish after it has applied.

10. Close the Exchange Management Console.

11. Click Start, All Programs, Microsoft Exchange Server 2007, and then click Exchange Management Shell.

12. At the Exchange Management Shell prompt, type **New-EmailAddressPolicy –Name 'External Mail Users and Contacts' –Priority 1 –EnabledEmailAddressTemplates 'SMTP:%g.%s-ext@StudentXX.com' –IncludedRecipients 'MailUsers,MailContacts'** and press Enter.

13. At the Exchange Management Shell prompt, type **Update-EmailAddressPolicy –Identity 'External Mail Users and Contacts'** and press Enter.

14. Close the Exchange Management Shell.

15. Click Start, All Programs, Microsoft Exchange Server 2007, and then click Exchange Management Console.

16. In the console tree pane, expand Recipient Configuration and highlight Mailbox.

17. Highlight Tiger Smith in the detail pane and click Properties in the action pane.

18. Highlight the E-Mail Addresses tab. Verify that Tiger Smith has received a primary email address of smitht@StudentXX.com and a secondary email address of tiger.smith@ StudentXX.com and click OK.

19. In the console tree pane, expand Recipient Configuration and highlight Mail Contact.

20. Highlight Courtney Davies in the detail pane and click Properties in the action pane.

21. Highlight the E-Mail Addresses tab. Verify that Courtney Davies has received a primary email address of courtney.davies-ext@StudentXX.com and click OK.

22. Close the Exchange Management Console.

Exercise 6.3	Configuring Messaging Records Management
Overview	Due to the sensitive nature of Project58, your organization has a legal responsibility to archive any emails sent to outside organizations regarding the details of the project for one year. You plan to implement a custom managed folder that will be applied to each Project58 member's mailbox that will retain messages for one year and remove them after that. In addition, Project58 members will be directed to copy any emails to external parties in regards to Project58 to this managed custom folder.
	For efficiency, you will use a bulk management command within the Exchange Management Shell to apply your managed folder mailbox policy to the appropriate mailbox users. In addition, to reduce the load on your

Mailbox role servers, you plan to run the Managed Folder Assistant only from 8:00 p.m. to 10:00 p.m. Monday to Friday.

To complete this lab exercise, StudentXX-A and StudentXX-B must be started and have network access.

Completion time	20 minutes

1. On StudentXX-A, log in as Administrator.

2. Click Start, All Programs, Microsoft Exchange Server 2007, and then click Exchange Management Console.

3. In the console tree pane, expand Organization Configuration and highlight Mailbox.

4. In the action pane, click New Managed Custom Folder.

5. At the New Managed Custom Folder window, type **Project58 Compliance** in the Name dialog box and note that the same name will be displayed in Outlook, Entourage, or OWA because it is also placed in the second dialog box.

6. Type **This folder contains emails related to Project58 for legal message compliance purposes** in the **Display the following comment when the folder is viewed in Outlook** dialog box.

7. Select **Do not allow users to minimize this comment in Outlook** and click New.

8. Click Finish to close the New Managed Custom Folder window.

9. Select the Managed Custom Folders tab in the detail pane, highlight Project58 Compliance, and select New Managed Content Settings in the action pane.

10. At the New Managed Content Settings window, type **Project58 Retention** in the Name dialog box and select E-mail from the Message type drop-down box.

11. Next, ensure that Length of retention period (days) is selected and type **365** in the associated dialog box.

12. Select **Delete and Allow Recovery** in the **Action to take at the end of the retention period** drop-down box and click Next.

13. At the Journaling page, click Next.

14. Review your settings and click New.

15. Click Finish to close the New Managed Content Settings window.

16. In the action pane, click New Managed Folder Mailbox Policy.

17. At the New Managed Folder Mailbox Policy window, type **Project58 Managed Folder Policy** in the Managed folder mailbox policy name dialog box.

18. Click Add, select the Project58 Compliance folder, and click OK.

19. Click New.

20. Click Finish to close the New Managed Folder Mailbox Policy window.

21. In the console tree pane, expand Server Configuration and highlight Mailbox.

22. In the detail pane, highlight StudentXX-A and click Properties in the action pane.

23. Select the Messaging Records Management tab, select **Use Custom Schedule** from the drop-down box, and click Customize.

24. Use your mouse to highlight the cells that represent 8:00 p.m. to 10:00 p.m. Monday to Friday (the cells will turn blue) and click OK.

25. Click OK to close StudentXX-A properties.

26. Perform the same procedure outlined in Steps 22 to 25 on StudentXX-B in the detail pane.

27. Close the Exchange Management Console.

28. Click Start, All Programs, Accessories, and then click Notepad.

29. Enter the following lines in Notepad:

    Identity
    "Sophia Boren"
    "Celine DeVries"
    "Mark Daly"
    "Meg Roombas"
    "Jessica Augustus"
    "Tom Hurt"
    "Bernadette Jones"
    "Matt Adams"
    "David Schwan"
    "Administrator"

30. Click File and then click Save. Type **"C:\Project58Members.csv"** in the File name dialog box (you must use the double quotes) and click Save.

31. Close Notepad.

32. Click Start, All Programs, Microsoft Exchange Server 2007, and then click Exchange Management Shell.

33. At the Exchange Management Shell prompt, type **Import-CSV 'C:\Project58 Members.csv' | ForEach-Object –Process { Set-Mailbox -Identity $_.Identity –Managed FolderMailboxPolicy 'Project58 Managed Folder Policy' }** and press Enter.

Question 3	*What is another method for configuring a managed folder mailbox policy for mailbox users?*

34. At the Exchange Management Shell prompt, type **Start-ManagedFolderAssistant -Identity StudentXX-A, StudentXX-B** and press Enter.

35. Close the Exchange Management Shell.

36. Click Start, All Programs, Microsoft Office, and then click Microsoft Office Outlook 2007.

37. Under Mailbox—Administrator in the left pane, expand Managed Folders and note the Project58 Compliance folder.

38. Highlight Inbox under Mailbox—Administrator in the left pane. Drag an existing email to the Project58 Compliance folder.

39. Close Outlook 2007.

Exercise 6.4	**Configuring Message Journaling**	
Overview	As part of your internal message compliance requirements, you wish to monitor all messages that are sent by mailbox users that have mailboxes within the Mailbox Database of the First Storage Group on StudentXX-B by copying them to a mailbox called journalarchive in the Mailbox Database within the First Storage Group on StudentXX-A using standard journaling.	
	In addition, you wish to monitor all messages sent to the Project-Managers mail-enabled universal security group. Any emails sent to this group should be copied to the Administrator mailbox using premium journaling.	
	To complete this lab exercise, StudentXX-A and StudentXX-B must be started and have network access.	
Completion time	15 minutes	

1. On StudentXX-A, log in as Administrator.

2. Click Start, All Programs, Microsoft Exchange Server 2007, and then click Exchange Management Console.

3. Using the procedures that you learned earlier in Lab 5.1, create a new mailbox user called Archive (First name = journalarchive, Last name = <blank>, Alias = journalarchive, Password = Secret123, Password should not expire) using the Mailbox Database within the First Storage Group on StudentXX-A.

4. In the console tree pane, expand Server Configuration and highlight Mailbox.

5. In the detail pane, select StudentXX-B, highlight the Mailbox Database in the First Storage Group within the work pane, and click Properties in the action pane.

6. On the General tab of Mailbox Database properties, select Journal Recipient, click the Browse button, select journalarchive, and click OK.

7. Click OK to close Mailbox Database properties.

8. In the console tree pane, expand Organization Configuration and highlight Hub Transport.

9. In the action pane, click New Journal Rule.

10. At the New Journal Rule window, type **Project Managers Journaling** in the Rule name dialog box.

11. Click Browse next to the Send journal reports to e-mail address dialog box, select Administrator, and click OK.

12. Select Journal messages for recipient and click Browse. Select the Project-Managers mail-enabled group and click OK.

13. Ensure that Enable Rule is selected and click New.

14. Click Finish to close the New Journal Rule window.

15. Close the Exchange Management Console.

16. Click Start, All Programs, Microsoft Office, and then click Microsoft Office Outlook 2007.

17. Click New and compose a new email to the Project-Managers group. When finished, send your email.

18. Highlight Inbox under Mailbox—Administrator in the left pane. View the journaled message.

Question 4	When you open the email, how is the original email message displayed?

19. Open the message attachment and read the contents.

20. Close all email message windows and close Outlook 2007.

Exercise 6.5	**Performing Bulk Management of Recipient Objects**
Overview	Your organization has two office locations within a few blocks of one another (King Street and Weber Street). Mailbox users primarily work in a single location. As a result, you wish to set the second custom attriute on all mailbox users to their primary location so that you can create additional address lists and dynamic distribution groups to match each location in the future.
	In addition, Project45 at your Weber Street location has grown dramatically in the past few months and requires the addition of several new project managers. You will need to configure mailbox users and the appropriate attributes, restrictions, and group membership for these new project managers.
	To simplify administration, you plan to use bulk management commands within the Exchange Management Shell to perform these tasks.
	To complete this lab exercise, StudentXX-A and StudentXX-B must be started and have network access.
Completion time	40 minutes

1. On StudentXX-A, log in as Administrator.

2. Click Start, All Programs, Accessories, and then click Notepad.

3. Enter the following lines in Notepad:

    Identity,Location
    "Sophia Boren","King Street"
    "Mel Booker","Weber Street"
    "Celine DeVries","Weber Street"
    "Mark Daly","King Street"
    "Tiger Smith","King Street"
    "Meg Roombas","King Street"
    "Jacques Guillere","Weber Street"
    "Juan Ton","Weber Street"
    "Sarah Parkers","Weber Street"
    "Lois Lipshitz","King Street"
    "Jessica Augustus","King Street"
    "Tom Hurt","King Street"
    "Bernadette Jones","King Street"
    "Jennifer Coupland","Weber Street"
    "Lisa Lackner","Weber Street"
    "Mathew Kropf","Weber Street"
    "Matt Adams","Weber Street"
    "David Schwan","Weber Street"

4. Click File and then click Save. Type **"C:\MailboxUsers.csv"** in the File name dialog box (you must use the double quotes) and click Save.

5. Close Notepad.

6. Click Start, All Programs, Microsoft Exchange Server 2007, and then click Exchange Management Shell.

7. At the Exchange Management Shell prompt, type **Import-CSV 'C:\MailboxUsers.csv' | ForEach-Object –Process { Set-Mailbox –Identity $_.Identity –CustomAttribute2 $_.Location }** and press Enter.

8. At the Exchange Management Shell prompt, type **Import-CSV 'C:\MailboxUsers.csv' | ForEach-Object –Process { Get-Mailbox –Identity $_.Identity | Select DisplayName,CustomAttribute2 | Format-List }** and press Enter. Verify that the correct values were set for Custom Attribute 2.

9. Close the Exchange Management Shell.

10. Click Start, All Programs, Accessories, and then click Notepad.

11. Enter the following lines in Notepad:

    Name,FirstName,LastName,UserPrincipalName,Alias
    "Dan Knot","Dan","Knot","dan.knot@StudentXX.com","dan.knot"
    "Joey Ranuy","Joey","Ranuy","joey.ranuy@StudentXX.com","joey.ranuy"
    "May Eby","May","Eby","may.eby@StudentXX.com","may.eby"
    "Sarah Dever","Sarah","Dever","sarah.dever@StudentXX.com","sarah.dever"
    "Harvey Kropf","Harvey","Kropf","harvey.kropf@StudentXX.com","harvey.kropf"

12. Click File and then click Save. Type **"C:\NewMailboxUsers.csv"** in the File name dialog box (you must use the double quotes) and click Save.

13. Close Notepad.

14. Click Start, All Programs, Microsoft Exchange Server 2007, and then click Exchange Management Shell.

15. At the Exchange Management Shell prompt, type **$password = Read-Host 'Enter password' –AsSecureString** and press Enter. Type **Secret123** when prompted and press Enter.

16. At the Exchange Management Shell prompt, type **Import-CSV 'C:\NewMailbox Users.csv' | ForEach-Object –Process { New-Mailbox –Name $_.Name –FirstName $_.FirstName –LastName $_.LastName –UserPrincipalName $_.UserPrincipalName –Alias $_.Alias –Database 'StudentXX-A\First Storage Group\Mailbox Database' – OrganizationalUnit 'StudentXX.com/Production' –Password $password –Reset PasswordOnNextLogon $true }** and press Enter.

Question 5	What would happen if you executed Step 16 without first executing Step 15?

17. At the Exchange Management Shell prompt, type **Import-CSV 'C:\NewMailbox Users.csv' | ForEach-Object –Process { Set-Mailbox –Identity $_.Name –Custom Attribute1 'Project45' –CustomAttribute2 'Weber Street' –MaxSendSize 2097152 –MaxReceiveSize 2097152 }** and press Enter.

Question 6	Briefly explain what Step 17 does.

18. At the Exchange Management Shell prompt, type **Import-CSV 'C:\NewMail boxUsers.csv' | ForEach-Object –Process { Add-DistributionGroupMember –Identity 'Project-Managers' –Member $_.Name }** and press Enter.

Question 7	Briefly explain what Step 18 does.

19. At the Exchange Management Shell prompt, type **Import-CSV 'C:\NewMailbox Users.csv'| ForEach-Object –Process { Get-Mailbox –Identity $_.Name } | Move-Mailbox –TargetDatabase 'StudentXX-B\First Storage Group\Mailbox Database'** and press Enter.

Question 8	Briefly explain what Step 19 does.

20. At the Exchange Management Shell prompt, type **Import-CSV 'C:\NewMailbox Users.csv' | ForEach-Object –Process { Get-Mailbox –Identity $_.Name } | Format-List** and press Enter. Verify that your previous commands correctly configured the appropriate settings for each mailbox user.

21. Close the Exchange Management Shell.

LAB REVIEW QUESTIONS

Completion time	15 minutes

1. Describe what you learned by completing this lab.

2. Explain why creating address lists improves the productivity of your users.

3. In Lab Exercise 6.2, why did you have to use the Exchange Management Shell to create the External Mail Users and Contacts email address policy?

4. In Lab Exercise 6.3, what would you modify to ensure that any emails that are forwarded to the Project58 Compliance folder are copied to an archive mailbox (e.g., archive@StudentXX.com)?

5. In Lab Exercise 6.4, you configured both standard and premium message journaling. Briefly explain when one type of message journaling is preferred over the other.

6. From your experience performing the steps in Lab Exercise 6.5, why is it best to use CSV files alongside bulk management commands?

LAB CHALLENGE 6.1: CONFIGURING ADDRESS LISTS USING THE EXCHANGE MANAGEMENT SHELL

Completion time	10 minutes

Now that your mailbox users have a second custom attribute that identifies their office location, you can create address lists to make it easier for users within your organization to locate recipients by office. Use the Exchange Management Shell to create a "King Street Office" address list and a "Weber Street Office" address list under the root of the address lists folder and apply your address list configuration.

LAB CHALLENGE 6.2: CREATING A POWERSHELL SCRIPT

Completion time	15 minutes

Your organization plans to increase its number of project managers in the next year for both Project45 and Project58. As a result, you will need to create additional mailbox users for them and configure them in much the same way that you did in Steps 10 to 21 of Lab Exercise 6.5.

To simplify administration, you would like to reuse the C:\NewMailboxUsers.csv file that you created in Steps 11 and 12 of Lab Exercise 6.5 and replace the user information with the information for future project managers. However, the mailbox database, OU, office, and project for each future project manager is unknown.

Create a PowerShell script called **C:\Program Files\Microsoft\Exchange Server\Scripts\ AddProjectManagers.ps1** that configures new project managers as described in Steps 10 to 21 of Lab Exercise 6.5. In addition, ensure that the PowerShell script accepts arguments that specify the CSV file, target mailbox database, target OU, office, and project for each group of project managers that needs to be added in the future. When finished, test your script using sample user information in the C:\NewMailboxUsers.csv file.

LAB 7
CONFIGURING PUBLIC FOLDERS

This lab contains the following exercises and activities:

Exercise 7.1	Configuring a Mail-Enabled Support Public Folder
Exercise 7.2	Creating Project Public Folders
Exercise 7.3	Configuring a Public Folder Home Page
Exercise 7.4	Configuring Public Folder Replicas
Lab Review Questions	
Lab Challenge 7.1	Configuring a Form for Public Folder Posts

BEFORE YOU BEGIN

Lab 7 assumes that setup has been completed as specified in the setup document and that StudentXX-A, StudentXX-B, and StudentXX-C have connectivity to the classroom network and the Internet. Moreover, Lab 7 assumes that you have completed the exercises in previous labs.

> **NOTE**
>
> *In this lab, you will see the characters XX. When you see these characters, substitute the two-digit number assigned to your computer.*

SCENARIO

To help centralize IT support and provide information sharing for Project45 users, you will implement the appropriate public folders on StudentXX-A and configure content replicas on StudentXX-B.

In the Lab Challenge, you will configure the public folder to use a custom form.

After completing this lab, you will be able to:

- Create and mail enable public folders

- Configure public folder permissions and features

- Configure moderated public folders

- Configure public folders using bulk management commands

- Configure public folder content replicas

Estimated lab time: 100 minutes

Exercise 7.1	Configuring a Mail-Enabled Support Public Folder
Overview	To simplify providing administrative support, you plan to create a Support mail-enabled public folder that MAPI clients can post items to or email when they need help. This folder should allow all internal and external users to post items but only allow Administrator to view and manage them. In addition, to alert Administrator of new entries, you should configure Administrator as the moderator for the Support public folder. You also wish to hide the mail-enabled public folder from Exchange address lists to prevent unnecesary emails. To complete this lab exercise, StudentXX-A and StudentXX-B must be started and have network access.
Completion time	20 minutes

1. On StudentXX-A, log in as Administrator.

2. Click Start, All Programs, Microsoft Exchange Server 2007, and then click Exchange Management Console.

3. In the console tree pane, highlight Tool box and double click Public Folder Management Console in the detail pane.

4. Expand Default Public Folders in the console tree pane and highlight Default Public Folders.

5. In the action pane, click New Public Folder.

6. At the New Public Folder window, type **Support** in the Name dialog box and click New.

7. Click Finish to close the New Mailbox window.

8. Expand Default Public Folders in the console tree pane and highlight Support in the detail pane.

9. In the action pane, click Mail Enable.

10. In the action pane, click Properties.

11. Highlight the Exchange General tab and select **Hide from Exchange address list**. Next, highlight the E-Mail Addresses tab and view the default email address.

Question 1	What is the default alias and email address used for your public folder?

12. Click OK to close public folder properties.

13. In the action pane, click Manage Send As Permission.

14. At the Manage Send As Permission window, click Add, select Administrator, and click OK.

15. Click Manage.

16. Click Finish and close the Public Folder Management Console and the Exchange Management Console.

17. Click Start, All Programs, Microsoft Office, and then click Microsoft Office Outlook 2007.

18. Under Public Folders in the left pane, expand All Public Folders, right click Support, and click Properties.

19. Highlight the Permissions tab of public folder properties. In the dialog box, highlight Default and select Contributor from the Permission Level drop-down dialog box.

Question 2	What type of access do internal and external senders have to the Support public folder?

Question 3	What type of access does Administrator have to the Support public folder?

20. Highlight the Administration tab and click the Moderated Folder button.

21. At the Moderated Folder window, select **Set folder up as a moderated folder**. Next, click To, select Administrator and click OK.

22. Select **Reply to new items**. Next, select Custom Response and click Template. When Outlook opens, type **IT Department Request Received** in the Subject dialog box and type **Thank you for your submission. You should receive a reply shortly regarding your problem. Be aware that it may take additional time to receive a response during times of high volume** in the body of the email.

23. Close the Outlook window and click Yes when prompted to save changes.

24. Next to the Moderators dialog box, click Add, select Administrator, and click OK.

25. Click OK to close the Moderated Folder window.

26. Click OK to close public folder properties.

27. Highlight Inbox under Mailbox—Tiger Smith in the left pane. Compose a new email from Tiger Smith to support@StudentXX.com. Observe the moderated folder autoreply that you receive.

28. Highlight Inbox under Mailbox—Administrator. View the email from Tiger Smith. Drag the email to the Support public folder for later use.

29. Close Outlook 2007.

Exercise 7.2	Creating Project Public Folders
Overview	The mailbox users that are members of Project45 must use public folders to coordinate and distribute journals and meeting notes as well as post project comments. Project45 members should be able to post and manage their own journal items as well as post and view their own meeting notes, but should only be allowed to post comments. Mel Booker is in charge of the public folder hierarchy and should be given the necessary permissions to administer it as well as post, view, and manage all items within the public folders.
	To satisfy these requirements, you plan to implement a public folder hierarchy for them with the necessary permissions for each user. To simplify permission assignments, you will use bulk management commands within the Exchange Management Shell.
	To complete this lab exercise, StudentXX-A and StudentXX-B must be started and have network access.
Completion time	30 minutes

1. On StudentXX-A, log in as Administrator.

2. Click Start, All Programs, Microsoft Office, and then click Microsoft Office Outlook 2007. The Microsoft Outlook window appears.

3. Click on the Folder List icon in the lower left pane. In the Folder List window, expand Public Folders, All Public Folders.

4. Right click All Public Folders and select New Folder.

5. At the Create New Folder window, type **Project45** in the Name dialog box. Select Mail and Post Items in the drop-down box and click OK.

6. Right click Project45 and select New Folder.

7. At the Create New Folder window, type **Journals** in the Name dialog box. Select Journal Items in the drop-down box and click OK.

8. Right click Project45 and select New Folder.

9. At the Create New Folder window, type **Comments** in the Name dialog box. Select Mail and Post Items in the drop-down box and click OK.

10. Right click Project45 and select New Folder.

11. At the Create New Folder window, type **Meeting Notes** in the Name dialog box. Select Mail and Post Items in the drop-down box and click OK.

12. Close Microsoft Outlook.

13. Click Start, All Programs, Accessories, and then click Notepad.

14. Enter the following lines in Notepad:

    Identity
    "Tiger Smith"
    "Jacques Guillere"
    "Juan Ton"
    "Sarah Parkers"
    "Lois Lipshitz"
    "Jennifer Coupland"
    "Lisa Lackner"
    "Mathew Kropf"

15. Click File and then click Save. Type **"C:\Project45Members.csv"** in the File name dialog box (you must use the double quotes) and click Save.

16. Close Notepad.

17. Click Start, All Programs, Microsoft Exchange Server 2007, and then click Exchange Management Shell.

18. At the Exchange Management Shell prompt, type **Import-CSV 'C:\Project45 Members.csv' | ForEach-Object –Process { Add-PublicFolderClientPermission – Identity '\Project45' –Server 'StudentXX-A' –User $_.Identity –AccessRights 'Reviewer' }** and press Enter.

Question 4	*What type of access does the Reviewer client permission grant to Project45 users for the Project45 public folder?*

19. At the Exchange Management Shell prompt, type **Import-CSV 'C:\Project45 Members.csv' | ForEach-Object –Process { Add-PublicFolderClientPermission – Identity '\Project45\Comments' –Server 'StudentXX-A' –User $_.Identity –Access Rights 'NonEditingAuthor' }** and press Enter.

Question 5	*What type of access does the NonEditingAuthor client permission grant to Project45 users for the Project45 public folder?*

20. At the Exchange Management Shell prompt, type **Import-CSV 'C:\Project45 Members.csv' | ForEach-Object –Process { Add-PublicFolderClientPermission – Identity '\Project45\Journals' –Server 'StudentXX-A' –User $_.Identity –Access Rights 'Author' }** and press Enter.

Question 6	*What type of access does the Author client permission grant to Project45 users for the Project45 public folder?*

21. At the Exchange Management Shell prompt, type **Import-CSV 'C:\Project45 Members.csv' | ForEach-Object –Process { Add-PublicFolderClientPermission – Identity '\Project45\Meeting Notes' –Server 'StudentXX-A' –User $_.Identity – AccessRights 'Contributor' }** and press Enter.

Question 7	*What type of access does the Contributor client permission grant to Project45 users for the Project45 public folder?*

22. Close the Exchange Management Shell.

23. Click Start, All Programs, Accessories, and then click Notepad.

24. Enter the following lines in Notepad:

    Folder
    "\Project45"
    "\Project45\Journals"
    "\Project45\Meeting Notes"
    "\Project45\Comments"

25. Click File and then click Save. Type **"C:\Project45Folders.csv"** in the File name dialog box (you must use the double quotes) and click Save.

26. Close Notepad.

27. Click Start, All Programs, Microsoft Exchange Server 2007, and then click Exchange Management Shell.

28. At the Exchange Management Shell prompt, type **Import-CSV 'C:\Project45 Folders.csv' | ForEach-Object –Process { Add-PublicFolderClientPermission – Identity $_.Folder –Server 'StudentXX-A' –User 'Mel Booker' –AccessRights 'Editor' }** and press Enter.

Question 8	What type of access does the Editor client permission grant to Mel Booker for the Project45 public folders?

29. At the Exchange Management Shell prompt, type **Import-CSV 'C:\Project45 Folders.csv' | ForEach-Object –Process { Add-PublicFolderAdministrative Permission –Identity $_.Folder –Server 'StudentXX-A' –User 'Mel Booker' –Access Rights 'AllExtendedRights' }** and press Enter.

Question 9	What type of access does the All Extended Rights administrative permission grant to Mel Booker for the Project45 public folders?

30. At the Exchange Management Shell prompt, type **Import-CSV 'C:\Project45 Folders.csv' | ForEach-Object –Process { Get-PublicFolderClientPermission – Identity $_.Folder –Server 'StudentXX-A' | Format-List }** and press Enter. Verify your client public folder permission assignments.

31. At the Exchange Management Shell prompt, type **Import-CSV 'C:\Project45 Folders.csv' | ForEach-Object –Process { Get-PublicFolderAdministrative Permission –Identity $_.Folder –Server 'StudentXX-A' | Format-List }** and press Enter. Verify your administrative public folder permission assignments.

32. Close the Exchange Management Shell.

Exercise 7.3	Configuring a Public Folder Home Page
Overview	Because the Project45 folder merely serves to organize the Comments, Journals, and Meeting Notes folders for Project45, you wish to attach a web page to the Project45 folder that describes the usage of the folders within. Before creating the web page, you wish to ensure that public folder users will see the web page when they highlight the Project45 public folder.
	To test this, you wish to configure the Project45 folder to use the homepage http://www.google.com and verify that the web page appears when you access the public folder using Outlook.
	To complete this lab exercise, StudentXX-A and StudentXX-B must be started and have network access.
Completion time	5 minutes

1. On StudentXX-A, log in as Administrator.

2. Click Start, All Programs, Microsoft Office, and then click Microsoft Office Outlook 2007. The Microsoft Outlook window appears.

3. Click on the Folder List icon in the lower left pane. In the Folder List window, expand Public Folders, All Public Folders, and Project45.

4. Right click the Project45 public folder and select Properties.

5. Highlight the Home Page tab, select **Show home page by default for this folder**, type **http://www.google.com** in the Address dialog box, and click OK.

6. Highlight the Project45 public folder in the left pane and verify that the correct web page is displayed.

7. Next, highlight the Journals public folder in the left pane and ensure that the web page is not displayed.

8. Close Microsoft Outlook.

Exercise 7.4	Configuring Public Folder Replicas
Overview	Some Project45 users complain that access to the Project45 public folders is quite slow. After investigation, you notice that these users are connecting to the public folder database on StudentXX-B and are redirected to the public folder database on StudentXX-A using public folder referrals.
	To allow Project45 users to access their public folders from either StudentXX-A or StudentXX-B, you plan to create a public folder replica on StudentXX-B that holds the Project45 folders that you created on StudentXX-A after working hours (8:00 a.m. to 6:00 p.m.). Moreover, to reduce the strain on public folder replication, you plan to configure the Project45 public folders to remove any items older than 14 days because Project45 items are no longer needed after two weeks.
	To complete this lab exercise, StudentXX-A and StudentXX-B must be started and have network access.
Completion time	10 minutes

1. On StudentXX-A, log in as Administrator.

2. Click Start, All Programs, Microsoft Exchange Server 2007, and then click Exchange Management Console.

3. In the console tree pane, highlight Tools and double click Public Folder Management Console in the detail pane.

4. Expand Default Public Folders in the console tree pane, highlight the Project45 public folder in the detail pane and click Properties in the action pane.

5. Highlight the Replication tab and click Add. Select the Public Folder Database on StudentXX-B and click OK.

6. Deselect **Use public folder database replication schedule** and click Customize. Highlight the cells that represent 8:00 a.m. to 6:00 p.m. Monday to Friday and click OK.

7. Type **14** in the **Local replica age limit** dialog box and highlight the Limits tab.

8. Deselect **Use database age defaults** and type **14** in the **Age limit for replicas (days)** dialog box.

9. Click OK.

10. Using the procedure outlined in Steps 4 to 9, ensure that the Comments, Journals, and Meeting Notes folders under the Project45 public folder are also replicated to the public folder database on StudentXX-B using the same schedule and restrictions.

11. Close the Public Folder Management Console and close the Exchange Management Console.

LAB REVIEW QUESTIONS

Completion time   15 minutes

1. Describe what you learned by completing this lab.

2. What is another way to configure your Exchange organization so that emails sent to support@StudentXX-com are sent to Administrator?

3. Explain why you could not use the Public Folder Management Console to create the Journal public folder in Lab Exercise 7.2.

4. What is the difference between the **Local replica age limit** and **Age limit for replicas** settings in Lab Exercise 7.4?

LAB CHALLENGE 7.1: CONFIGURING A FORM FOR PUBLIC FOLDER POSTS

Completion time   20 minutes

Project45 users post comments regularly to the Project45\Comments public folder. To standardize the information that is included within the Project45\Comments public folder, you wish to create a custom form that includes fields to identify the nature of the comment as well as the area of Project45 that it applies to.

Create a new custom form based on a standard post item that satisfies these requirements and ensure that new post items in the Project45\Comments public folder use this form by default. When finished create a new post in the Project45\Comments public folder to test your configuration.

LAB 8
CONFIGURING PROTOCOLS AND TRANSPORT RULES

This lab contains the following exercises and activities:

Exercise 8.1	Configuring POP3 and IMAP4
Exercise 8.2	Configuring HTTP
Exercise 8.3	Configuring the Autodiscover and Availability Services for Outlook Anywhere
Exercise 8.4	Configuring SMTP
Exercise 8.5	Configuring a Transport Rule
Lab Review Questions	
Lab Challenge 8.1	Configuring Additional Transport Rules

BEFORE YOU BEGIN

Lab 8 assumes that setup has been completed as specified in the setup document and that StudentXX-A, StudentXX-B, and StudentXX-C have connectivity to the classroom network and the Internet. Moreover, Lab 8 assumes that you have completed the exercises in previous labs.

NOTE	*In this lab, you will see the characters XX. When you see these characters, substitute the two-digit number assigned to your computer.*

94

SCENARIO

Now that you have configured the appropriate recipient objects and policies, you need to ensure that the client access protocols on your CAS role servers are correctly configured to allow for client access within your organization as well as configure client access protocol restrictions. In addition, you will need to configure a transport rule on your Hub role server to alter the processing of email to match company needs.

In the Lab Challenge, you will configure additional transport rules on the Hub and Edge role servers within your organization.

After completing this lab, you will be able to:

- Configure the POP3, IMAP4, HTTP, and Outlook Anywhere protocols on a CAS role server

- Configure the SMTP protocol on a Hub role server

- Configure transport rules on Hub and Edge role servers

Estimated lab time: 120 minutes

Exercise 8.1	Configuring POP3 and IMAP4
Overview	Although your organization allows both POP3 and IMAP4 connections for email retrieval from outside the organization, POP3 is only used by a small number of older email clients and some wireless portable devices that do not support TLS and rich text formats. IMAP4 is the recommended protocol for accessing email outside of the organization and is used by many organization members from their email clients at home.
	As a result, you plan to configure your POP3 and IMAP4 services accordingly. In addition, you plan to limit the number of POP3 connections to 50 and the number of IMAP4 connections to 500 for each CAS role server to reflect the number of POP3 and IMAP4 clients that you expect to have in the next year.
	To complete this lab exercise, StudentXX-A and StudentXX-B must be started and have network access.
Completion time	15 minutes

1. On StudentXX-A, log in as Administrator.

2. Click Start, All Programs, Microsoft Exchange Server 2007, and then click Exchange Management Console.

3. In the console tree pane, expand Server Configuration and select Client Access.

4.   Select StudentXX-A in the detail pane and highlight the POP3 and IMAP4 tabs in the work pane.

5.   In the work pane, highlight POP3 and click Properties in the action pane.

6.   Highlight the Binding tab.

> **Question 1** *What are the default ports used for POP3, POP3+TLS, and POP3+SSL?*

7.   Highlight the Authentication tab.

> **Question 2** *What is the default authentication method used for POP3?*

8.   Select **Plain text logon**.

9.   Highlight the Connection tab and enter **50** in the **Maximum connections** and **Maximum connections from a single IP address** dialog boxes.

10. Click OK.

11. Click in the work pane, highlight IMAP4, and click Properties in the action pane.

12. Highlight the Binding tab.

> **Question 3** *What are the default ports used for IMAP4, IMAP4+TLS, and IMAP4+SSL?*

13. Highlight the Authentication tab and note the default authentication method of TLS.

14. Highlight the Connection tab and enter **500** in the **Maximum connections** and **Maximum connections from a single IP address** dialog boxes.

15. Using the procedure outlined in Steps 4 through 14, configure the POP3 and IMAP4 protocols on StudentXX-B.

16. Close the Exchange Management Console.

17. Click Start, All Programs, Administrative Tools, and then click Services.

18. Right click Microsoft Exchange POP3 and click Restart.

19. Right click Microsoft Exchange IMAP4 and click Restart.

20. Close the Services console.

21. On StudentXX-B, log in as Administrator.

22. Using the procedure outlined in Steps 17 through 20, restart the POP3 and IMAP4 services on StudentXX-B.

Exercise 8.2	Configuring HTTP
Overview	Your organization also allows the use of OWA for access email internally and externally when other methods are unavailable. However, by default, OWA forces users to type StudentXX.com\username at the OWA logon screen.
	You must ensure that OWA is configured to allow for internal and external access for up to 200 concurrent connections per CAS role server as well as ensure that users only need to type their username at the OWA logon screen (their domain name should be automatically supplied).
	To complete this lab exercise, StudentXX-A and StudentXX-B must be started and have network access.
Completion time	15 minutes

1. On StudentXX-A, log in as Administrator.

2. Click Start, All Programs, Microsoft Exchange Server 2007, and then click Exchange Management Console.

3. In the console tree pane, expand Server Configuration and select Client Access.

4. Select StudentXX-A in the detail pane and highlight the Outlook Web Access tab in the work pane.

5. Highlight owa (Default Web Site) in the work pane and click Properties in the action pane.

6. Ensure that **https://StudentXX-A.StudentXX.com** is entered in the Internal URL and External URL dialog boxes to provide for internal and external access to OWA.

7. Highlight the Authentication tab and ensure that **Use form-based authentication** is selected. Next, select User name only, click the Browse button, select StudentXX.com, and click OK. Close the warning box.

8. Click OK to close owa (Default Web Site) properties.

9. Using the procedure outlined in Steps 4 to 8, configure StudentXX-B to use the URL **https://StudentXX-B.StudentXX.com** for internal and external requests as well as ensure that users only need to type their username in the OWA logon box.

Question 4	*What must happen before the OWA changes that you made take effect?*

10. Close the Exchange Management Console.

11. Click Start, All Programs, Administrative Tools, and then click Internet Information Services (IIS) Manager.

12. At the Internet Information Services (IIS) Manager window, expand StudentXX-A, Web sites in the left pane.

13. Right click Default Web Site and click Properties.

14. Highlight the Performance tab, select **Connections limited to**, and enter **200** in the dialog box.

15. Click OK to close Default Web Site Properties.

16. Right click StudentXX-A in the left pane, select All Tasks, and click Restart IIS.

17. Close the Internet Information Services (IIS) Manager console.

18. On StudentXX-B, log in as Administrator.

19. Using the procedure outlined in Steps 11 to 17, configure the Default Web Site on StudentXX-B to allow a maximum of 200 concurrent connections and restart IIS on StudentXX-B.

Exercise 8.3	Configuring the Autodiscover and Availability Services for Outlook Anywhere
Overview	Your organiation has decided to allow those users who have Outlook 2007 on their home computer to access their company email using Outlook Anywhere. To simplify configuration and management of Outlook Anywhere, you plan to configure the Autodiscover and Availability services on your CAS role servers to allow for Outlook Anywhere clients and test the connectivity settings afterward.
	To complete this lab exercise, StudentXX-A and StudentXX-B must be started and have network access.
Completion time	15 minutes

1. On StudentXX-A, log in as Administrator.

2. Click Start, All Programs, Microsoft Exchange Server 2007, and then click Exchange Management Shell.

3. At the Exchange Management Shell prompt, type **Set-OutlookAnywhere -Identity 'StudentXX-A' -ExternalHostname 'StudentXX-A.StudentXX.com'** and press Enter.

4. At the Exchange Management Shell prompt, type **Set-OutlookAnywhere -Identity 'StudentXX-B' -ExternalHostname 'StudentXX-B.StudentXX.com'** and press Enter.

5. At the Exchange Management Shell prompt, type **Set-OABVirtualDirectory -Identity 'StudentXX-A\OAB (Default Web Site)' -ExternalURL 'https://StudentXX-A.StudentXX.com' -RequireSSL:$true** and press Enter.

6. At the Exchange Management Shell prompt, type **Set-OABVirtualDirectory -Identity 'StudentXX-B\OAB (Default Web Site)' -ExternalURL 'https://StudentXX-B.StudentXX.com' -RequireSSL:$true** and press Enter.

7. At the Exchange Management Shell prompt, type **Set-WebServicesVirtualDirectory -Identity 'StudentXX-A\EWS (Default Web Site)' -ExternalURL 'https://StudentXX-A.StudentXX.com/EWS/Exchange.asmx' -BasicAuthentication:$true** and press Enter.

8. At the Exchange Management Shell prompt, type **Set-WebServicesVirtualDirectory -Identity 'StudentXX-B\EWS (Default Web Site)' -ExternalURL 'https://StudentXX-B.StudentXX.com/EWS/Exchange.asmx' -BasicAuthentication:$true** and press Enter.

9. At the Exchange Management Shell prompt, type **Test-OutlookWebServices – ClientAccessServer 'StudentXX-A.StudentXX.com' | Format-List** and press Enter. Observe your test results.

10. At the Exchange Management Shell prompt, type **Test-OutlookWebServices –Client AccessServer 'StudentXX-B.StudentXX.com' | Format-List** and press Enter. Observe your test results.

11. Close the Exchange Management Shell.

Exercise 8.4	Configuring SMTP
Overview	To allow for SMTP relay from the POP3 and IMAP4 clients within your organization, you have implemented the appropriate send and receive connectors in Lab 4. Because StudentXX-A hosts four server roles (Mailbox, Hub, CAS, and UM), you would like to ensure that SMTP relay does not exceed 500 concurrent outbound connections on the server.
	Additionally, you must also prevent out-of-office replies, delivery reports, and nondelivery reports to all external domains. However, one of your partner organizations, Initech Inc. (initech.com), requires out-of-office replies, delivery reports, and nondelivery reports. Moreover, any emails sent to Initech must not use Exchange rich text format.
	To complete this lab exercise, StudentXX-A and StudentXX-B must be started and have network access.
Completion time	10 minutes

1. On StudentXX-A, log in as Administrator.

2. Click Start, All Programs, Microsoft Exchange Server 2007, and then click Exchange Management Console.

3. In the console tree pane, expand Server Configuration and highlight Hub Transport.

4. Highlight StudentXX-A in the detail pane and click Properties in the action pane.

5. Highlight the Limits tab, enter **500** in the **Maximum concurrent outbound connections** dialog box and click OK.

6. In the console tree pane, expand Organization Configuration and highlight Hub Transport.

7. Highlight the Remote Domains tab in the detail pane, select Default in the work pane, and click Properties from the action pane.

8. On the General tab of the Default remote domain properties, click **Allow none**.

9. Highlight the **Format of original message sent as attachment to journal report** tab, deselect **Allow non-delivery reports** and **Allow delivery reports**, and click OK.

10. In the action pane, click New Remote Domain.

11. At the New Remote Domain window, type **Initech** in the Name dialog box and type **initech.com** in the Domain name dialog box. Next, select **Include all subdomains** and click New.

12. Click Finish to close the New Remote Domain window.

13. Select Initech in the work pane and click Properties from the action pane.

14. Click **Allow external out-of-office messages and out-of-office messages sent by Outlook 2003 or earlier clients or sent by Exchange Server 2003 or earlier servers**.

15. Highlight the **Format of original message sent as attachment to journal report** tab, select **Never use** in the Exchange rich text format section, and click OK.

16. Close the Exchange Management Console.

Exercise 8.5	Configuring a Transport Rule
Overview	For legal purposes, external communication regarding Project45 and Project58 should be minimized within your organization. Any emails sent to external recipients regarding Project45 and Project58 should contain a legal disclaimer that identifies the confidential nature of the information included within. This legal disclaimer should be appended to the email with a separator line using a medium-size blue font. In addition, a copy of these external project emails must be sent to Administrator for auditing purposes.
	To comply with these requirements, you plan to create a transport rule on the Hub role servers within your organization.
	To complete this lab exercise, StudentXX-A, StudentXX-B, and StudentXX-C must be started and have network access.
Completion time	20 minutes

1. On StudentXX-A, log in as Administrator.

2. Click Start, All Programs, Microsoft Exchange Server 2007, and then click Exchange Management Console.

3. In the console tree pane, expand Organization Configuration and highlight Hub Transport.

4. In the action pane, click New Transport Rule.

5. At the New Transport Rule window, type **External Project Emails** in the Name dialog box, and type **This transport rule appends a legal disclaimer to all external Project45 and Project58 emails as well as sends a copy of these emails to Administrator for auditing** in the Comment dialog box.

6. Verify that Enable Rule is selected to ensure that the transport rule is enabled after creation and click Next.

7. In the **Step 1: Select condition(s)** section, select **sent to users inside or outside the organization**.

8. In the **Step 2: Edit the rule description by clicking an underlined value** click the **Inside** underlined word. In the Select scope window that appears, select Outside from the drop-down box and click OK.

9. In the **Step 1: Select condition(s)** section, select **when the Subject field or the body of the message contains specific words**.

10. In the **Step 2: Edit the rule description by clicking an underlined value** section, click the **specific words** underlined words. In the Specify words window that appears, type **Project45** and click Add. Next, type **Project58**, click Add, and click OK.

11. Click Next.

12. In the **Step 1: Select action(s)** section on the Actions page, select append disclaimer text using font, size, color, with separator, and fallback to action if unable to apply.

Question 5	*What is the default configuration of the disclaimer text shown in the Step 2: Edit the rule description by clicking an underlined value dialog box?*

13. In the **Step 2: Edit the rule description by clicking an underlined value** section, click the **disclaimer text** underlined words. In the Select disclaimer text window that appears, type the following text in the Disclaimer text dialog box and click OK.

This transmission (including any attachments) may contain confidential information, privileged material (including material protected by the solicitor-client or other applicable privileges), or constitute nonpublic information. Any use of this information by anyone other than the intended recipient is prohibited. If you have

received this transmission in error, please immediately reply to the sender and delete this information from your system. Use, dissemination, distribution, or reproduction of this transmission by unintended recipients is not authorized and may be unlawful.

14. Click the **smallest** underlined word. In the Select font size window that appears, select Normal from the drop-down box and click OK.

15. Click the **Gray** underlined word. In the Select font color window that appears, select Blue from the drop-down box and click OK.

16. In the **Step 1: Select action(s)** section of the Actions page, select **Blind carbon copy (Bcc) the message to addresses**.

17. In the **Step 2: Edit the rule description by clicking an underlined value** section, click the **addresses** underlined word. In the Select recipients text window that appears, click Add, select Administrator, and click OK.

18. Click OK again to return to the Actions page and click Next.

19. At the Exceptions page, click Next.

20. At the Create Rule page, click New.

21. Click Finish to close the New Transport Rule window.

22. Close the Exchange Management Console.

23. Click Start, All Programs, Microsoft Office, and then click Microsoft Office Outlook 2007.

24. In the left pane of Outlook 2007, expand Mailbox—Tiger Smith and highlight Inbox.

25. Click New to compose a new email.

26. Click the From button and select Tiger Smith.

27. In the To field, type **someperson@somedomain.com**. Type **Transport Rule Test** in the Subject field. Type **Project45 information** in the body and click the Send button.

28. Expand Mailbox—Administrator in the left pane of Outlook 2007 and highlight Inbox. Double click the related email from Tiger Smith to verify that your transport rule was applied.

29. Close the email and Outlook 2007.

LAB REVIEW QUESTIONS

Completion time	15 minutes

1. Describe what you learned by completing this lab.

2. Explain why it is important to limit the number of concurrent client connections on your CAS role servers.

3. After configuring the Availability and Autodiscover services for Outlook Anywhere clients in Lab Exercise 8.3, what must you do to ensure that Outlook Anywhere clients can access the CAS role servers within your organization?

4. Why is it important to configure remote domains on your Hub role servers?

5. Why did you not need to configure the transport rule on StudentXX-B in Lab Exercise 8.5?

LAB CHALLENGE 8.1: CONFIGURING ADDITIONAL TRANSPORT RULES

Completion time	30 minutes

In addition to the transport rule that you have configured in Lab Exercise 8.5, configure an additional transport rule on your Hub role servers that sends a copy of all messages to Administrator that are marked with the "Extremely Confidential" custom message classification. You must first ensure that custom message classification is created. In addition, you must add the custom message classification to your Outlook 2007 client on StudentXX-A and test your configuration.

Following this, create a transport rule on your Edge role server that automatically deletes any emails with a Spam Confidence Level (SCL) of eight or greater.

LAB 9
CONFIGURING SECURITY

This lab contains the following exercises and activities:

Exercise 9.1   Reducing the Edge Role Attack Surface

Exercise 9.2   Configuring Antispam Agents

Exercise 9.3   Configuring Forefront Security for Exchange

Exercise 9.4   Configuring CA-Signed Certificates for Protocol Encryption

Exercise 9.5   Implementing User Certificates

Lab Review Questions

Lab Challenge 9.1   Configuring a Block List Provider

BEFORE YOU BEGIN

Lab 9 assumes that setup has been completed as specified in the setup document and that StudentXX-A, StudentXX-B, and StudentXX-C have connectivity to the classroom network and the Internet. Moreover, Lab 9 assumes that you have completed the exercises in previous labs.

> **NOTE**
>
> *In this lab, you will see the characters XX. When you see these characters, substitute the two-digit number assigned to your computer.*

SCENARIO

To provide security for your Exchange infrastructure, you will need to configure the appropriate technologies. For your Edge role server, you plan to use the Security Configuration Wizard

(SCW) to stop unnecessary services and implement Windows Firewall. In addition, you plan to configure antispam agents on your Edge role server to reduce incoming Internet spam as well as install and configure Forefront Security for Exchange (FSE) to minimize viruses that are sent to your organization.

To provide better security on the other Exchange servers within your organization, you plan to replace the default self-signed certificates used for SSL and TLS with CA-signed certificates from an Enterprise CA. Moreover, this Enterprise CA will also be used to sign user certificates used for email encryption and signing.

In the Lab Challenge, you will configure a block list provider on your Edge role server.

After completing this lab, you will be able to:

- Use the SCW to configure services and firewall settings

- Configure the antispam agents on an Edge role server

- Install and configure Forefront Security for Exchange

- Install and configure an Enterprise CA

- Configure CA-signed certificates for use by IMAP4, POP3, UM, HTTP, and SMTP

- Deploy and configure user certificates for email encryption and signing

Estimated lab time: 170 minutes

Exercise 9.1	Reducing the Edge Role Attack Surface
Overview	Because StudentXX-C is located in the public DMZ network within your organization, you wish to reduce its attack surface by disabling unnecessary services and restricting access to ports using Windows Firewall. To identify and configure the appropriate settings, you plan to use the Security Configuration Wizard (SCW) component of Windows.

To complete this lab exercise, StudentXX-C must be started and have network access. |
| Completion time | 20 minutes |

1. On StudentXX-C, log in as the local Administrator account.

2. Click Start, Control Panel, and then click Add or Remove Programs. When the Add or Remove Programs window appears, click Add/Remove Windows Components to open the Windows Components Wizard.

3. On the Windows Components page, select Security Configuration Wizard and click Next.

4. Click Finish to close the Windows Components Wizard. Close the Add or Remove Programs window.

5. Click Start and then click Run.

6. In the Run dialog box, type **scwcmd register /kbname:Ex2007KB /kbfile:"%program files%\Microsoft\Exchange Server\Scripts\Exchange2007.xml"** and click OK.

Question 1	*What does the scwcmd command do?*

7. Click Start, Administrative Tools, and then click Security Configuration Wizard. When the Security Configuration Wizard window appears, click Next.

8. At the Configuration Action screen, ensure that **Create a new security policy** is selected and click Next.

9. At the Select Server screen, click Browse, select StudentXX-C, and click OK.

10. When finished, click Next.

11. After a few moments, click View Configuration Database to open the SCW Viewer window. View the information regarding Edge role services, close the SCW Viewer, and click Next.

12. At the Role-Based Service Configuration page, click Next.

13. At the Select Server Roles page, deselect **File Server** and click Next.

14. At the Select Client Features page, deselect **DHCP client** and click Next.

15. At the Select Administration and Other Options page, click Next.

16. At the Additional Services page, click Next.

17. At the Handling Unspecified Services page, ensure that **Do not change the startup mode of the service** is selected and click Next.

18. At the Confirm Service Changes window, review the proposed changes to the existing services on your computer and click Next.

19. At the Network Security Configuration page, click Next.

20. At the Open Ports and Approve Applications page, review the open ports and click Next.

21. At the Confirm Port Configuration page, review the port selections for Windows Firewall and click Next.

22. At the Registry Settings page, select Skip this section and click Next.

23. At the Audit Policy page, select Skip this section and click Next.

24. At the Internet Information Services page, select Skip this section and click Next.

25. At the Save Security Policy page, click Next.

26. At the Security Policy File Name page, type **C:\SCW-Edge.xml** in the Security policy file name dialog box and click Next.

Question 2	*What can the C:\SCW-Edge.xml file be used for?*

27. Click OK to close the information window.

28. Select Apply now and click Next.

29. Click Next and then click Finish to close the Security Configuration Wizard.

30. Reboot StudentXX-C.

Exercise 9.2	Configuring Antispam Agents
Overview	The Edge role server in your organization is partially configured by default to reduce spam within your organization. To maximize the antispam effectiveness of your Edge role server, you plan to configure antispam agents on your Edge role server to reject emails that are addressed to blank senders or senders not listed in the Global Address List and to reject emails that have restricted attachments or are considered spam using sender ID or reputation filtering.
	In addition, your organization has experienced a large number of spam messages that largely consist of messages with the phrase "special offer" from senders within the greatdeals.com domain. After checking protocol logs, you notice that these emails are relayed from the IP address 12.7.1.5. You wish to prevent these spam emails from reaching recipients as soon as possible.
	Moreover, any email messages that have a Spam Confidence Level (SCL) of 9 should be deleted and any email messages with an SCL of 8 should be rejected and the sender notified. Any email messages with an SCL of 7 should be forwarded to a spam mailbox (spam@StudentXX.com) for later viewing.
	To complete this lab exercise, StudentXX-A, StudentXX-B, and StudentXX-C must be started and have network access.
Completion time	15 minutes

1. On StudentXX-A, log in as Administrator.

2. Click Start, All Programs, Microsoft Exchange Server 2007, and then click Exchange Management Console.

3.   In the console tree pane, expand Recipient Configuration and highlight Mailbox.

4.   In the action pane, click New Mailbox.

5.   At the New Mailbox window, select User Mailbox and click Next.

6.   Select New user and click Next.

7.   At the User Information page, type **spam** in the Name and User logon name dialog boxes, type **Secret123** in both password dialog boxes, and click Next.

8.   Click Browse next to the Mailbox database dialog box, select the Mailbox Database in the First Storage Group on StudentXX-A, and click OK.

9.   Click Next. Review the summary of your settings and click New.

10. Click Finish to close the New Mailbox window.

11. Close the Exchange Management Console.

12. On StudentXX-C, log in as Administrator.

13. Click Start, All Programs, Microsoft Exchange Server 2007, and then click Exchange Management Console.

14. In the console tree pane, select Edge Transport and highlight the Anti-spam tab in the work pane.

15. Select Content Filtering in the work pane and click Properties in the action pane.

16. In the Content Filtering Properties window, highlight the Custom Words tab, type **special offer** in the lower dialog box and click Add.

17. Highlight the Action tab. Type **9** in the **Delete messages that have an SCL rating greater than or equal to**, type **8** in the **Reject messages that have an SCL rating greater than or equal to**, type **7** in the **Quarantine messages that have an SCL rating greater than or equal to**, type **spam@StudentXX.com** in the **Quarantine mailbox e-mail address** dialog box, and click OK.

18. Select IP Block List in the work pane and click Properties in the action pane.

19. Highlight the Blocked Addresses tab, click Add, and ensure that any emails relayed from the IP address **12.7.1.5** are blocked indefinitely. Click OK when finished and click OK to close the IP Block List window.

20. Select Recipient Filtering in the work pane and click Properties in the action pane.

21. Highlight the Blocked Recipients tab, ensure that **Block messages sent to recipients not listed in the Global Address List** is selected and click OK.

Question 3	Why is it a good practice to filter messages that are not addressed to recipients in the Global Address List?

22. Select Sender Filtering in the work pane and click Properties in the action pane.

23. Highlight the Blocked Senders tab, ensure that **Block messages from blank senders** is selected. Click Add and ensure that any emails from users within the **greatdeals.com** domain are blocked and click OK.

24. Highlight the Action tab, ensure that Reject message is selected, and click OK.

25. Select Sender ID in the work pane and click Properties in the action pane.

26. Highlight the Action tab, ensure that Reject message is selected, and click OK.

Question 4	What does Sender ID filtering use to detect spam messages?

27. Select Sender Reputation in the work pane and click Properties in the action pane.

28. Highlight the Sender Confidence tab and ensure that **Perform an open proxy test when determining sender confidence level** is selected.

Question 5	What does an open proxy test help identify?

29. Highlight the Action tab, select a threshold of **6** using the slider, type **48** in the dialog box, and click OK.

Question 6	What will happen to emails that are below the sender confidence threshold?

30. Close the Exchange Management Console.

31. Click Start, All Programs, Microsoft Exchange Server 2007, and then click Exchange Management Shell.

32. At the Exchange Management Shell prompt, type **Get-AttachmentFilterEntry** and press Enter. View the list of filtered attachments.

33. At the Exchange Management Shell prompt, type **Get-AttachmentFilterListConfig** and press Enter.

Question 7	What is the default action for emails that have restricted attachments?

34. At the Exchange Management Shell prompt, type **Set-AttachmentFilterListConfig –Action Reject –RejectResponse "Your email has been rejected by StudentXX.com due to an unacceptable attachment."** and press Enter.

35. Close the Exchange Management Shell.

Exercise 9.3	Configuring Forefront Security for Exchange
Overview	To provide for virus detection for inbound email from the Internet, you have decided to install and configure Forefront Security for Exchange (FSE) on the Edge role server (StudentXX-C).
	To complete this lab exercise, StudentXX-C must be started and have network access. In addition you must first download a 120-day evaluation copy of FSE from the Microsoft Web site.
Completion time	25 minutes

1. On StudentXX-C, log in as the local Administrator account.

2. Navigate to the folder that contains the 120-day evaluation of FSE that you downloaded or the folder that contains the licensed copy of FSE and double click setup.exe. When the Welcome page appears, click Next.

3. On the License Agreement page, click Yes.

4. On the Customer Information page, enter your name and company in the appropriate dialog boxes and click Next.

5. On the Installation Location page, ensure that Local Installation is selected and click Next.

6. On the Installation Type page, ensure that Full Installation is selected and click Next.

7. At the Quarantine Security Settings page, click Next.

8. At the Engines page, select four more antivirus engines of your choice and click Next.

Question 8	Which engine is selected by default?

9. At the Engines Updates Required page, read the update information and click Next.

10. At the Proxy Server page, click Next.

11. At the Choose Destination Location page, click Next.

12. At the Select Program Folder page, click Next.

13. At the Start Copying Files page, click Next.

14. At the Restart Exchange Transport Service page, click Next to restart the Exchange Transport Service to activate Forefront.

15. At the Recycling Exchange Transport Service page, click Next.

16. Click Finish to close the FSE setup window.

17. Reboot StudentXX-C and log in as the local Administrator account.

18. Click Start, All Programs, Microsoft Forefront Server Security, Exchange Server, and then click Forefront Server Security Administrator.

Question 9	Which scan job is enabled by default?

19. Under the Settings section in the left pane of FSE, select Antivirus.

20. Select **Max Certainty** in the Bias drop-down box.

21. Select **Delete: remove infection** in the Action drop-down box.

22. Under the Settings section in the left pane of FSE, select General Options and ensure that the **Scan on scanner update** option is selected.

Question 10	What does the Scan on scanner update option do?

23. Under the Settings section in the left pane of FSE, select Scanner Updates and click Update Now.

24. Close Forefront Server Security Administrator.

Exercise 9.4	Configuring CA-Signed Certificates for Protocol Encryption
Overview	To enhance the security of your Exchange organization, you wish to replace the default self-signed certificate used for SSL and TLS connections with a CA-signed certificate.
	To achieve this, you plan to install a CA on StudentXX-A and issue the CA trusted root certificate to all domain computers. Next, you will use IIS Manager to remove the existing certificate and enroll for a CA-signed certificate for StudentXX-A and StudentXX-B. Finally, you must ensure that the CA-signed certificate is used for IMAP4, POP3, UM, HTTP, and SMTP.
	To complete this lab exercise, StudentXX-A and StudentXX-B must be started and have network access.
Completion time	60 minutes

1. On StudentXX-A, log in as Administrator.

2. Click Start, Control Panel, and then click Add or Remove Programs. When the Add or Remove Programs window appears, click Add/Remove Windows Components to open the Windows Components Wizard.

3. On the Windows Components page, select Certificate Services and click Yes.

Question 11	What restriction is placed on your computer when it becomes a CA?

4. Click Next.

5. At the CA Type page, ensure that Enterprise root CA is selected and click Next.

6. At the CA Identifying Information page, type **StudentXX_CA** in the Common name for this CA dialog box.

Question 12	How long is the CA public and private key pair valid for by default and what does this signify?

7. Click Next.

8. At the Certificate Database Settings page, click Next. When prompted to stop IIS to complete the installation of Certificate Services, click Yes.

9. Insert your Windows Server 2003 CD-ROM when prompted. When prompted to enable ASP, click Yes.

10. Click Finish to close the Windows Components Wizard window.

11. Click Start, Administrative Tools, and then click Active Directory Users and Computers.

12. Right click StudentXX.com in the left pane and click Properties.

13. At the domain properties window, highlight the Group Policy tab, select Default Domain Policy, and click Edit.

14. In the left pane of the Group Policy Object Editor, navigate to Default Domain Policy > Computer Configuration > Windows Settings > Security Settings > Public Key Policies > Trusted Root Certification Authorities.

15. Right click Trusted Root Certification Authorities in the left pane and click Import. When the Certificate Import Wizard appears, click Next.

16. On the File to Import page, click Browse, navigate to C:\, select StudentXX-A. StudentXX.com_StudentXX_CA.crt, and click OK.

17. Click Next.

18. On the Certificate Store page, click Next.

19. Click Finish to close the Certificate Import Wizard. Click OK to close the information dialog box.

20. Close the Group Policy Object Editor.

21. Click OK to close the domain Properties window and close the Active Directory Users and Computers window.

22. Click Start, Administrative Tools, and then click Internet Information Services (IIS) Manager.

23. In the left pane of Internet Information Services (IIS) Manager, expand StudentXX-A and then expand Web Sites. Right click Default Web Site and select Properties.

24. At the Default Web Site Properties window, highlight the Directory Security tab and click Server Certificate.

25. At the Web Server Certificate Wizard window, click Next.

26. On the Modify the Current Certificate Assignment page, select **Remove the current certificate** and click Next.

27. Review the details of the certificate that you are removing and click Next.

28. Click Finish to close the IIS Certificate Wizard.

29. In the Default Web Site Properties window, click Server Certificate.

30. At the Web Server Certificate Wizard window, click Next.

31. On the Modify the Current Certificate Assignment page, ensure that **Create a new certificate** is selected and click Next.

32. At the Delayed or Immediate Request page, ensure that **Send the request immediately to an online certification authority** is selected and click Next.

33. On the Name and Security Settings page, type **StudentXX-A.StudentXX.com** in the Name dialog box.

34. On the Organization Information page, type **StudentXX** in the Organization dialog box, type **HeadOffice** in the Organizational unit dialog box, and click Next.

35. On the Your Site's Common Name page, enter **StudentXX-A.StudentXX.com** in the Common name dialog box and click Next.

Question 13	*Why is it important to remember the name that you type in the Common name dialog box?*

36. On the Geographical Information page, supply the appropriate information about your Exchange server's physical location in the appropriate drop-down or dialog boxes (Choose your own geographic location) and click Next when finished.

37. On the SSL Port page, ensure that port 443 is listed in the dialog box and click Next.

38. On the Choose a Certification Authority page, select StudentXX_CA from the Certification authorities drop-down box and click Next.

39. On the Certificate Request Submission page, review your certificate request settings and click Next.

40. Click Finish to close the IIS Certificate Wizard.

41. In the Default Web Site Properties window, click Edit under the Secure communications section. Ensure that **Require secure channel (SSL)** and **Require 128-bit encryption** is selected and click OK.

42. Click OK to close the Default Web Site Properties window and close IIS Manager.

43. Click Start, All Programs, Microsoft Exchange Server 2007, and then click Exchange Management Shell.

44. At the Exchange Management Shell prompt, type **Get-ExchangeCertificate** and press Enter.

Question 14	*What is the Subject name of the default self-signed certificate for StudentXX-A called?*

Question 15	*What is the Subject name of the CA-signed certificate for StudentXX-A called?*

Question 16	*Is the CA-signed certificate used for all of the available services and protocols (IPUWS in the Services column)?*

45. Write down the thumbprint for the CA-signed certificate for StudentXX-A.

46. At the Exchange Management Shell prompt, type **Enable-ExchangeCertificate -Thumbprint** *thumbprint* **-Services 'IMAP, POP, UM, IIS, SMTP'** and press Enter where *thumbprint* is the thumbprint that you recorded in the previous step.

47. At the Exchange Management Shell prompt, type **Get-ExchangeCertificate** and press Enter. Verify that the CA-signed certificate is configured for use with all protocols and services.

48. Close the Exchange Management Shell.

49. On StudentXX-B, log in as Administrator.

50. Using the procedure outlined in Steps 22 to 48, configure a CA-signed certificate for use with the protocols and services on StudentXX-B (use **StudentXX-B.StudentXX.com** instead of StudentXX-A.StudentXX.com).

Exercise 9.5	Implementing User Certificates
Overview	Several users within your organization have requested email encryption within their Outlook clients. Before deploying user certificates to these users, you plan to test the configuration of user certificates using your own user account.
	To complete this lab exercise, StudentXX-A and StudentXX-B must be started and have network access.
Completion time	10 minutes

1. On StudentXX-A, log in as Administrator.

2. Click Start and click Run. In the run dialog box, type **certtmpl.msc** and press Enter.

3. In the right pane of the Certificate Templates window, right click User and click Properties. On the Security tab, ensure that Authenticated Users is allowed the Read and Enroll permissions.

4. Close the Certificate Templates window.

5. Click Start and click Run. In the run dialog box type **certmgr.msc** and press Enter.

6. In the left pane of the Certificates—Current User window, expand Personal and Certificates.

7. Right click Certificates, select All Tasks, and click Request New Certificate.

8. At the Certificate Request Wizard window, click Next.

9. On the Certificate Types page, select User and click Next.

10. On the Certificate Friendly Name and Description page, type **Outlook Certificate** in the Friendly name dialog box and click Next.

11. Click Finish to close the Certificate Request Wizard.

12. Click OK to close the result dialog box and view the user certificate listed in the right pane of the Certificate—Current User window.

Question 17	*Where is the user certificate stored?*

13. Close the Certificates—Current User window.

14. Click Start, All Programs, Microsoft Office, and then click Microsoft Office Outlook 2007.

15. Click the Tools menu and select Trust Center.

16. At the Trust Center window, click E-mail Security in the left pane and select the **Encrypt contents and attachments for outgoing messages** and **Add digital signature to outgoing messages** options.

17. Click Settings, ensure that Outlook Certificate is listed in the Signing Certificate and Encryption Certificate dialog boxes and click OK.

18. Click OK to close the Trust Center window.

19. In the left pane of Outlook 2007, expand Mailbox—Administrator and highlight Inbox.

20. Click New to compose a new email.

21. Click the To button, select Administrator and click OK. Type **Certificate Test** in the Subject field. Type **Email body** in the body and click the Send button.

22. View your new email and note that the contents and digital signature were validated successfully.

23. Close the email and Outlook 2007.

LAB REVIEW QUESTIONS

Completion time	15 minutes

1. Describe what you learned by completing this lab.

2. Why should you use the SCW to configure system service startup and Windows Firewall when both of these tasks can be performed using the Services Console and Network Properties?

3. In Lab Exercise 9.2, why did you configure attachment filtering using the Exchange Management Shell?

4. Why is it a good practice to install at a minimum Forefront Security for Exchange on the Edge role servers within your organization?

5. Briefly explain why you should replace the default self-signed SSL/TLS certificate with a CA-signed certificate?

6. In Lab Exercise 9.4, why did you need to configure the Default Domain Policy?

7. Explain the benefits and disadvantages of using a larger number of bits when generating a certificate.

8. In Lab Exercise 9.5, what would happen if you tested the user certificate for Administrator in Outlook by sending a message from Administrator to Tiger Smith?

LAB CHALLENGE 9.1: CONFIGURING A BLOCK LIST PROVIDER

Completion time	15 minutes

Using the Internet, research free block list providers that can be configured within Exchange Server 2007. Next, configure your Edge role server (StudentXX-C) to use this provider using the Exchange Management Shell.

LAB 10
BACKING UP, RESTORING, AND REPAIRING EXCHANGE

This lab contains the following exercises and activities:

Exercise 10.1	Performing a Full Backup of a Storage Group
Exercise 10.2	Restoring a Storage Group Backup
Exercise 10.3	Restoring a Deleted Item
Exercise 10.4	Using the Recovery Storage Group
Exercise 10.5	Defragmenting and Repairing Exchange Databases
Lab Review Questions	
Lab Challenge 10.1	Backing Up Server Roles

BEFORE YOU BEGIN

Lab 10 assumes that setup has been completed as specified in the setup document and that StudentXX-A, StudentXX-B, and StudentXX-C have connectivity to the classroom network and the Internet. Moreover, Lab 10 assumes that you have completed the exercises in previous labs.

> **NOTE**
>
> *In this lab, you will see the characters XX. When you see these characters, substitute the two-digit number assigned to your computer.*

SCENARIO

To protect the data and configuration within your Exchange infrastructure, you will need to perform regular backups of your Exchange servers as well as understand the practices and procedures that may be used to recover data.

In this lab, you will back up and restore Exchange information using a variety of different techniques to understand the Exchange backup and restore process. In a production environment, you will create a backup plan and use the information presented within this Lab on a repetitive basis for several Exchange servers.

Additionally, you will defragment a database in this lab to ensure fast access and minimize the chance of corruption as well as repair database corruption using command line utilities.

In the Lab Challenge, you will back up the configuration of your Exchange servers to protect against server failure.

After completing this lab, you will be able to:

- Back up Exchange Server 2007 databases

- Back up an Exchange Server 2007 configuration

- Restore a database backup and rebuild the search index

- Restore deleted items

- Create a Recovery Storage Group

- Use a Recovery Storage Group to restore mailboxes

- Perform a dial tone recovery using a Recovery Storage Group

- Inspect, defragment, and repair Exchange databases

Estimated lab time: 100 minutes

Exercise 10.1	Performing a Full Backup of a Storage Group
Overview	One of the most common backup/restore tasks that you will perform within an organization is backing up Exchange databases. Although public folders may contain important information, they can be replicated among Mailbox role servers for fault tolerance. As a result, the most common database backup that you will perform is a mailbox database backup.
	In addition, most organizations today use fast hard disk and network media as the target for backup jobs instead of tapes. Consequently, full backup types are typically chosen for these backups.

(*continued*)

> In this exercise, you will perform a full backup of a storage group that contains a mailbox database for later use in this Lab.
>
> To complete this lab exercise, StudentXX-A must be started and have network access.

Completion time	10 minutes

1. On StudentXX-A, log in as Administrator.

2. Click Start, All Programs, Accessories, System Tools, and then click Backup. If the Backup or Restore Wizard window appears, deselect Always start in wizard mode and click the Advanced Mode link.

3. At the Backup Utility window, highlight the Backup tab. In the left pane, expand Microsoft Exchange Server, StudentXX-A, and Microsoft Information Store.

4. Next, place a checkmark next to First Storage Group.

5. Type **C:\Backup1.bkf** in the **Backup media or file name** dialog box.

6. Click Start Backup.

7. At the Backup Job Information window, click Advanced.

Question 1	*What backup type is chosen by default?*

8. Click OK to close the Advanced Backup Options window.

9. Select **Replace the data on the media with this backup** and click Start Backup.

10. When the backup completes, click Report to view the backup log file.

Question 2	*Where would you look for this backup log after closing the Windows Backup utility?*

11. Close Notepad and click Close to close the Backup Progress window.

12. Close the Windows Backup utility.

13. Click Start, All Programs, Microsoft Exchange Server 2007, and then click Exchange Management Shell.

14. At the Exchange Management Shell prompt, type **Get-EventLog Application | where { $_.EventID –eq 8001 } | Format-List** and press Enter. Note the event that indicates that your recent backup job finished successfully.

15. Close the Exchange Management Shell.

Exercise 10.2	Restoring a Storage Group Backup
Overview	In this exercise, you will practice a full restore of a mailbox database from a full backup. This procedure is normally performed on a database that has experienced corruption. After the restore operation has completed, you will rebuild the search index to match the restored database contents.
	To verify the restoration process, you will examine changes to the Tiger Smith mailbox. Tiger Smith's mailbox will be restored as part of the mailbox database restoration.
	To complete this lab exercise, StudentXX-A and StudentXX-B must be started and have network access.
Completion time	15 minutes

1. On StudentXX-A, log in as Administrator.

2. Click Start, All Programs, Microsoft Office, and then click Microsoft Office Outlook 2007.

3. In the left pane of Outlook 2007, expand Mailbox—Tiger Smith and highlight Inbox.

4. Remove one of the emails in Tiger Smith's Inbox.

5. Close Outlook 2007.

6. Click Start, All Programs, Microsoft Exchange Server 2007, and then click Exchange Management Console.

7. In the console tree pane, expand Server Configuration and highlight Mailbox.

8. In the detail pane, select StudentXX-A. Next, highlight the Mailbox Database under the First Storage Group in the work pane and select Dismount Database from the action pane.

9. Click Yes when prompted to confirm the dismount operation.

10. Close the Exchange Management Console.

11. Click Start, All Programs, Accessories, System Tools, and then click Backup.

12. The Backup Utility window appears.

13. Highlight the Restore and Manage Media tab. In the left pane, expand File, Backup1.bkf and place a checkmark next to the backup of the First Storage Group. Note that both the Mailbox Database and Log Files are selected in the right pane.

14. Click Start Restore.

15. Ensure that StudentXX-A is listed in the Restore To dialog box, type **C:\temp** in the **Temporary location for log and patch files** dialog box, and select **Last Restore Set**.

 What does the Last Restore Set option do?

16. Click OK. When the restore operation has completed, click Close to close the Restore Progress window.

17. Close the Windows Backup utility.

18. Click Start, All Programs, Microsoft Exchange Server 2007, and then click Exchange Management Console.

19. In the console tree pane, expand Server Configuration and highlight Mailbox.

20. In the detail pane, select StudentXX-A. Next, highlight the Mailbox Database under the First Storage Group in the work pane and select Mount Database from the action pane.

21. Close the Exchange Management Console.

22. Click Start, All Programs, Microsoft Exchange Server 2007, and then click Exchange Management Shell.

23. At the Exchange Management Shell prompt, type **ResetSearchIndex.ps1 'First Storage Group\Mailbox Database'** and press Enter. Type **A** and press Enter to accept all modifications.

 Why did you run the ResetSearchIndex.ps1 after the restore operation?

24. Close the Exchange Management Shell.

25. Click Start, All Programs, Microsoft Office, and then click Microsoft Office Outlook 2007.

26. In the left pane of Outlook 2007, expand Mailbox—Tiger Smith and highlight Inbox. Note that the email that you deleted from Tiger Smith's Inbox is present.

27. Close Outlook 2007.

Exercise 10.3   Restoring a Deleted Item

Overview	Users can restore deleted items from their mailbox provided that they are recovered within a deleted item retention time frame.
	In this exercise, you will examine the deleted item retention time frame and use Outlook 2007 to recover a deleted item.
	To complete this lab exercise, StudentXX-A and StudentXX-B must be started and have network access.
Completion time	5 minutes

1. On StudentXX-A, log in as Administrator.

2. Click Start, All Programs, Microsoft Exchange Server 2007, and then click Exchange Management Console.

3. In the console tree pane, expand Server Configuration and highlight Mailbox.

4. In the detail pane, select StudentXX-A. Next, highlight the Mailbox Database under the First Storage Group in the work pane and select Properties from the action pane.

5. Highlight the Limits tab.

Question 5	*How long are deleted items retained by default?*

6. Click OK to close Mailbox Database Properties.

7. Close the Exchange Management Console.

8. Click Start, All Programs, Microsoft Office, and then click Microsoft Office Outlook 2007.

9. In the left pane of Outlook 2007, expand Mailbox—Administrator and highlight Inbox.

10. Right click one of your emails and click Delete.

11. Highlight Deleted Items under Mailbox—Administrator in the left pane.

12. Locate the same email that you removed from your Inbox, right click that email, and click Delete. When prompted to confirm the deletion, click Yes.

13. Highlight Deleted Items under Mailbox—Administrator in the left pane, click the Tools menu, and select Recover Deleted Items.

14. At the Recover Deleted Items window, select your email and click the Recover Selected Items icon (second icon from the left). Close the Recover Deleted Items window when finished.

15. Highlight Deleted Items under Mailbox—Administrator in the left pane.

Question 6	Is your previously deleted email present and why?

16. Drag your previously deleted email to the Inbox folder under Mailbox—Administrator in the left pane.

17. Close Outlook 2007.

Exercise 10.4	Using the Recovery Storage Group
Overview	The Recovery Storage Group (RSG) is a powerful and flexible tool for use when restoring information from backups. For deleted items that cannot be recovered as described in Lab Exercise 10.3, you can mount an RSG that is linked to the appropriate mailbox database, restore a backup to the RSG, and restore the necessary items to the mailbox using a copy/merge operation.
	RSGs can also be used to provide for quick recovery in the event that a mailbox database fails. To provide for quick recovery, you can mount an RSG that is linked to the appropriate mailbox database, restore a recent backup to the RSG, and swap the failed and RSG databases in a "dial tone" scenario.
	In this exercise, you will mount an RSG and restore a backup to it. Following this, you will restore a single mailbox from the RSG using a copy/merge operation as well as perform a dial tone recovery by swapping the RSG and original database paths.
	To complete this lab exercise, StudentXX-A and StudentXX-B must be started and have network access.
Completion time	20 minutes

1. On StudentXX-A, log in as Administrator.

2. Click Start, All Programs, Microsoft Exchange Server 2007, and then click Exchange Management Console.

3. In the console tree pane, highlight Toolbox. In the detail pane, double click Database Recovery Management under the Disaster recovery tools section.

4. When the Microsoft Exchange Troubleshooting Assistant window appears, enter **RSG Restoration 1** in the dialog box at the top of the window, ensure that StudentXX-A is listed in the Exchange server name and Domain controller name dialog boxes, and click Next.

5. Click **Create a recovery storage group**.

6. Highlight First Storage Group and click Next.

7. Type **Recovery Storage Group 1** in the Recovery storage group name dialog box.

Question 7	*What is the original path for the storage group and database files?*

Question 8	*What is the default path for the RSG?*

8. Click Create the recovery storage group. At the Create the Recovery Storage Group Result page, review the summary and click **Go back to task center**.

9. Minimize the Microsoft Exchange Troubleshooting Assistant window.

10. Click Start, All Programs, Accessories, System Tools, and then click Backup.

11. At the Backup Utility window, highlight the Restore and Manage Media tab. In the left pane, expand File, Backup1.bkf and place a checkmark next to the First Storage Group. Although Windows Backup indicates that the backup will be restored to the original location, it will be restored to the RSG that is linked to the First Storage Group instead.

12. Click Start Restore.

13. Ensure that StudentXX-A is listed in the Restore To dialog box and type **C:\temp** in the **Temporary location for log and patch files** dialog box.

14. Select **Last Restore Set** to ensure that the log files are replayed following the restore operation and click OK.

15. When the restore operation has completed, click Close to close the Restore Progress window.

16. Close the Windows Backup utility.

17. Maximize the Microsoft Exchange Troubleshooting Assistant window.

18. Select Mount or dismount databases in the recovery storage group.

19. At the Mount or Dismount Database page, select Mailbox Database and click Mount selected database.

20. After the database has been mounted, click **Go back to task center**.

21. Click **Merge or copy mailbox contents**.

22. Ensure that Mailbox Database is selected and click **Gather merge information**.

23. Click **Perform pre-merge tasks**.

24. Deselect all mailboxes except for Tiger Smith and click **Perform merge actions**.

25. Once the copy/merge operation has completed, click **Go back to task center**.

26. Select **Swap databases for 'dial-tone' scenario**.

27. Ensure that Mailbox Database is selected and click **Gather swap information**.

28. Review the file paths that will be changed and click **Perform swap action**.

29. Close the Microsoft Exchange Troubleshooting Assistant window and return to the Exchange Management Console.

30. In the console tree pane, expand Server Configuration and highlight Mailbox.

31. Select StudentXX-A in the detail pane and expand First Storage Group in the work pane. Highlight the First Storage Group in the work pane and click Refresh in the action pane.

Question 9	*What path is listed next to the Mailbox Database under the First Storage Group?*

32. Close the Exchange Management Console.

Exercise 10.5 Defragmenting and Repairing Exchange Databases

Overview	Sometimes, database corruption can be prevented or repaired using the eseutil.exe or isinteg.exe utilities. In this exercise, you will inspect, defragment, and repair a mailbox database using the eseutil.exe and isinteg.exe utilities.
	To complete this lab exercise, StudentXX-A must be started and have network access.
Completion time	10 minutes

1. On StudentXX-A, log in as Administrator.

2. Click Start, All Programs, Microsoft Exchange Server 2007, and then click Exchange Management Shell.

3. At the Exchange Management Shell prompt, type **Dismount-Database -Identity 'StudentXX-A\Third Storage Group\Second Mailbox Database'** and press Enter.

4. Close the Exchange Management Shell.

5. Click Start, All Programs, Accessories, and click Command Prompt. At the Windows command prompt, type **eseutil.exe /g 'C:\SG3\Second Mailbox Database.edb'** and press Enter.

Question 10	What does the /g option of eseutil.exe do?

6. At the Windows command prompt, type **eseutil.exe /d 'C:\SG3\Second Mailbox Database.edb'** and press Enter.

Question 11	What does the /d option of eseutil.exe do?

7. At the Windows command prompt, type **eseutil.exe /p 'C:\SG3\Second Mailbox Database.edb'** and press Enter. Read the warning and click Cancel.

Question 12	What does the /p option of eseutil.exe do and why is it not recommended for use on a database that is not damaged?

8. At the Windows command prompt, type **isinteg.exe –s StudentXX-A –fix –test alltests** and press Enter. Observe the menu that is displayed.

9. Type the number that corresponds to the Second Mailbox Database in the Third Storage Group (it should be marked as offline) and press Enter.

10. Type **y** and press Enter to perform the tests. Observe the results.

Question 13	What will happen if isinteg.exe detects errors and why?

11. Close the Windows command prompt.

12. Click Start, All Programs, Microsoft Exchange Server 2007, and then click Exchange Management Shell.

13. At the Exchange Management Shell prompt, type **Mount-Database -Identity 'StudentXX-A\Third Storage Group\Second Mailbox Database'** and press Enter.

14. Close the Exchange Management Shell.

LAB REVIEW QUESTIONS

Completion time   15 minutes

1. Describe what you learned by completing this lab.

2. When would you perform incremental backups of Exchange databases?

3. In practice, what should you do to ensure that users can recover their own deleted items within the deleted item retention time frame?

4. In addition to recovering mailbox data and performing dial tone recoveries, what is another use for the RSG?

5. Why is the isinteg.exe utility better to use on a corrupted database than the /p option to the eseutil.exe utility?

LAB CHALLENGE 10.1: BACKING UP SERVER ROLES

Completion time	**25 minutes**

Backing up databases on a Mailbox role server will protect against the failure of a database or the removal of data. However, you should also protect the configuration of your Exchange server roles to ensure that a server failure can be quickly restored in order to minimize downtime for your organization's Exchange infrastructure. In addition, several server roles maintain logs that should also be backed up to ensure that important information can be obtained following a server failure.

Using the information from Lesson 10, select the appropriate data to back up on StudentXX-A, StudentXX-B, and StudentXX-C according to their installed server roles (do not include mailbox or public folder databases). Next, back up this data using the appropriate utilities on each server.

LAB 11
MONITORING EXCHANGE

This lab contains the following exercises and activities:

Exercise 11.1	Monitoring Performance
Exercise 11.2	Monitoring Email Queues
Exercise 11.3	Tracking Messages
Exercise 11.4	Monitoring Client Connectivity
Exercise 11.5	Creating Usage Reports
Lab Review Questions	
Lab Challenge 11.1	Creating Server Reports

BEFORE YOU BEGIN

Lab 11 assumes that setup has been completed as specified in the setup document and that StudentXX-A, StudentXX-B, and StudentXX-C have connectivity to the classroom network and the Internet. Moreover, Lab 11 assumes that you have completed the exercises in previous labs.

> **NOTE**
>
> *In this lab, you will see the characters XX. When you see these characters, substitute the two-digit number assigned to your computer.*

SCENARIO

Monitoring the Exchange servers in your organization can be a large and daunting task. However, it is a necessary one to ensure that you can identify performance, email relay, and capacity problems before they occur as well as troubleshoot current problems. In addition, regular server monitoring is required for capacity planning and report generation.

In this lab, you will use a variety of different utilities to monitor server performance, email relay queues, message tracking logs, client connectivity, and server usage.

In the Lab Challenge, you will generate a server report that identifies four different aspects of your Exchange infrastructure.

After completing this lab, you will be able to:

- Use standard Windows utilities (Task Manager, System Monitor, Performance Logs and Alerts, Event Viewer) to monitor system performance

- Use the Exchange Best Practices Analyzer and Exchange Performance Troubleshooter to monitor and troubleshoot system performance

- Configure event logging levels for different Exchange components

- Monitor and troubleshoot email queues using various utilities

- Perform message tracking

- Monitor client connectivity using Outlook, protocol-related cmdlets, and SMTP protocol logs

- Create protocol, mailbox, and queue usage reports

- Create server reports

Estimated lab time: 200 minutes

Exercise 11.1	Monitoring Performance
Overview	In this exercise, you will examine the performance of StudentXX-A using various utilities (Task Manager, System Monitor, Performance Logs and Alerts, Event Viewer, Exchange Best Practices Analyzer, Exchange Performance Troubleshooter).
	The procedures in this exercise are designed to allow you to explore the various utilities available to Exchange Server 2007 for monitoring performance only and are not meant as a template for analyzing the performance of production Exchange server.
	To complete this lab exercise, StudentXX-A and StudentXX-B must be started and have network access.
Completion time	50 minutes

1.   On StudentXX-A, log in as Administrator.

2.   Press the Ctrl, Shift, and Esc keys simultaneously to start Task Manager.

3.   Highlight the Performance tab.

Question 1	*What could a high CPU Usage indicate and what would you do next?*

Question 2	*What could a high PF Usage indicate and what would you do next?*

4.   Highlight the Processes tab and click the CPU column twice to sort processes by highest CPU usage. Examine the output for possible rogue processes. Next, click the Mem Usage column twice to sort processes by highest memory usage and examine the output for rogue processes.

5.   Close Task Manager.

6.   Click Start, All Programs, Microsoft Exchange Server 2007, and then click Exchange Management Console.

7.   In the console tree pane, highlight Toolbox. In the detail pane, double click Performance Monitor under the Performance tools section.

8.   When System Monitor opens, note the default performance counters that are added to monitor your Exchange server.

9.   Click the Add icon (+), select MSExchangeIS Mailbox in the Performance object drop-down box, highlight Client Logons in the list of available counters, and click Add.

Question 3	*What does the Client Logons counter from the MSExchangeIS Mailbox performance object measure?*

10. Click Close to return to System Monitor.

11. Select the View Report icon.

12. Right click the report and click Save As. Type **C:\StudentXX-A Report** in the File name dialog box and click Save.

13. Close the Exchange Server Performance Monitor window and close the Exchange Management Console.

14. Click Start and then click My Computer. Navigate to **C:** and double click StudentXX-A.htm. If Internet Explorer restricts access to the web page, right click the message bar and select Allow Content. Examine the output.

15. Close Internet Explorer.

16. Click Start, Administrative Tools, Performance. When the Performance window appears, highlight Performance Logs and Alerts in the left pane.

17. In the right pane, right click Counter Logs and click New Log Settings.

18. In the New Log Settings window, type **Client Connection Monitoring** counter log and click OK.

19. At the counter log window, click Add Counters, select MSExchangeIS Mailbox in the Performance object drop-down box, highlight Client Logons in the list of available counters, and click Add.

20. Click Close to return to the counter log window.

21. Type **1** in the Interval dialog box to ensure that measurements are taken every second.

22. Highlight the Log Files tab.

Question 4	*What file is used to store the counter log by default?*

23. Click OK to create the counter log and start monitoring.

24. Minimize the Performance window.

25. Click Start, All Programs, Microsoft Office, and then click Microsoft Office Outlook 2007.

26. Close Outlook 2007.

27. Repeat the previous two steps several times. After one minute, return to the Performance window.

28. Expand Counter Logs in the left pane, right click Client Connection Monitoring in the right pane, and select Stop.

29. Click System Monitor in the left pane and remove all existing counters using the Delete icon (X).

30. Click the Add icon (+), select MSExchangeIS Mailbox in the Performance object drop-down box, highlight Client Logons in the list of available counters, and click Add.

31. Click the View Log Data icon.

32. At the System Monitor Properties window, select Log files and click Add. Navigate to C:\PerfLogs\Client Connection Monitoring_000001.blg and click Open.

33. Click OK to view the data from your counter log.

34. In the left pane, expand Performance Logs and Alerts.

35. Right click Alerts and click New Alert Settings.

36. In the New Alert Settings window, type **Client Connection Alert** and click OK.

37. At the alert window click Add, select MSExchangeIS Mailbox in the Performance object drop-down box, highlight Client Logons in the list of available counters, and click Add.

38. Ensure that Over is selected in the **Alert when the value is** dialog box and type **300** in the Limit dialog box.

39. Type **15** in the Interval dialog box to ensure that measurements are taken every 15 seconds.

40. Highlight the Action tab.

Question 5	*What will happen by default when the Client Logons counter is over 300?*

41. Click OK to create and activate your alert.

42. Click Start, All Programs, Microsoft Exchange Server 2007, and then click Exchange Management Shell.

43. At the Exchange Management Shell prompt, type **Get-EventLogLevel** and press Enter. Examine the output.

Question 6	*What is the default logging level used by most Exchange components when recording information within the Application event log?*

44. At the Exchange Management Shell prompt, type **Set-EventLogLevel –Identity 'MsExchange IMAP4\General' -Level 'High'** and press Enter.

45. At the Exchange Management Shell prompt, type **Set-CASMailbox –Identity 'Administrator' –IMAPEnabled $false** and press Enter to disable IMAP4 access for Administrator.

46. Close the Exchange Management Shell.

47. Click Start, All Programs, and then Outlook Express.

48. Ignore any warnings and close all Outlook Express windows.

49. Click Start, All Programs, Administrative Tools, and then Event Viewer.

50. Highlight Application in the left pane. Double click any warning messages from the MSExchangeIMAP4 source. One message should indicate that the Administrator user attempted to access IMAP4 but is disabled for that protocol.

51. Close Event Viewer.

52. Click Start, All Programs, Microsoft Exchange Server 2007, and then click Exchange Management Shell.

53. At the Exchange Management Shell prompt, type **Set-CASMailbox –Identity 'Administrator' –IMAPEnabled $true** and press Enter to reenable IMAP4 access for Administrator.

54. Close the Exchange Management Shell.

55. Click Start, All Programs, Microsoft Exchange Server 2007, and then click Exchange Management Console.

56. In the console tree pane, highlight Toolbox. In the detail pane, double click Best Practices Analyzer under the Configuration Management tools section.

57. At the Microsoft Exchange Best Practices Analyzer, click **Go to welcome screen**.

58. Click **Select options for a new scan**.

59. Ensure that StudentXX-A is listed in the Active Directory Server dialog box and click **Connect to the Active Directory server**.

60. Type **Performance Health Check** in the dialog box at the top of the window and ensure that Health Check is selected.

61. Deselect StudentXX-B in the scope dialog box and click Start scanning.

62. When the scan has completed, click **View a report of this Best Practices scan**.

63. Examine the results and performance suggestions.

64. Close the Microsoft Exchange Best Practices Analyzer window and return to the Exchange Management Console.

65. In the detail pane, double click Performance Troubleshooter under the Performance tools section.

66. At the Microsoft Exchange Troubleshooting Assistant, type **Test Performance Troubleshooting** in the dialog box and click Next.

67. Ensure that **Multiple users are complaining of delays while using Outlook . . .** is selected in the symptoms drop-down box and click Next.

68. Ensure that StudentXX-A is listed in the Server Name and global Catalog Server Name dialog boxes and click Next.

69. Ensure that C:\Perflogs is listed in the Root data directory dialog box and click Next to start collecting data.

70. Once the data has been collected and analyzed, the Performance Troubleshooter may ask you for additional information and perform additional scans based on the nature of your answers as well as the hardware and software on your Exchange server. Supply the appropriate information to the Performance Troubleshooter and examine the performance results at each stage of the process. When finished, close the Microsoft Exchange Troubleshooting Assistant window.

Exercise 11.2 Monitoring Email Queues

Overview	The regular monitoring of email queues is a key task for any Exchange administrator and is used to identify and troubleshoot email relay problems.
	In this exercise, you will send an email to a recipient in an invalid domain and to a recipient whose mailbox database is not mounted so that you can view the results in the Queue Viewer utility and by using cmdlets within the Exchange Management Shell. In addition, you will run the Mail Flow Troubleshooter to help identify the problem. Afterward, you will ensure that the emails are removed from the queue.
	To complete this lab exercise, only StudentXX-A and StudentXX-B must be started and have network access.
Completion time	20 minutes

1. On StudentXX-A, log in as Administrator.

2. Click Start, All Programs, Microsoft Exchange Server 2007, and then click Exchange Management Shell.

3. At the Exchange Management Shell prompt, type **Dismount-Database -Identity 'StudentXX-A\Third Storage Group\Second Mailbox Database'** and press Enter.

4. Close the Exchange Management Shell.

5. Click Start, All Programs, Microsoft Office, and then click Microsoft Office Outlook 2007.

6. In the left pane of Outlook 2007, expand Mailbox—Administrator and highlight Inbox.

7. Click New to compose a new email. Click the To button, select Meg Roombas and click OK. The mailbox for Meg Roombas is within the Second Mailbox Database in the Third Storage Group on StudentXX-A.

8. Type **Queue Test 1** in the Subject dialog box and click Send.

9. Click New to compose a new email. In the To dialog box, type **fakeuser@faketest domain.org**.

10. Type **Queue Test 2** in the Subject dialog box and click Send.

11. Close Outlook 2007.

12. Click Start, All Programs, Microsoft Exchange Server 2007, and then click Exchange Management Console.

13. In the console tree pane, highlight Toolbox. In the detail pane, double click Queue Viewer under the Mail flow tools section. Examine the output.

Question 7	*What queues are displayed and what messages are in each one?*

14. Highlight the Messages tab. View the details of each message and note the messages that have a Subject of Queue Test 1 or Queue Test 2.

15. Close the Queue Viewer.

16. In the detail pane, double click Mail Flow Troubleshooter under the Mail flow tools section.

17. At the Microsoft Exchange Troubleshooting Assistant window, type **Queue Troubleshooting** in the dialog box and select **Messages are backing up in one or more queues on a server** and click Next.

18. Ensure that StudentXX-A is listed in the Server Name and global Catalog Server Name dialog boxes and click Next.

19. At the Basic Server Information page, examine the information and warnings shown for your server and click Next.

20. At the Initial Queue Analysis Results page, examine the information and warnings shown for your queues and click Next. Depending on the contents of your queues, you may be required to press Next to perform additional tests.

21. On the View Results page, examine the possible causes for message queue problems.

Question 8	*Did the Mail Flow Troubleshooter identify the cause of the problem?*

22. When finished, close the Microsoft Exchange Troubleshooting Assistant window and close the Exchange Management Console.

23. Click Start, All Programs, Microsoft Exchange Server 2007, and then click Exchange Management Shell.

24. At the Exchange Management Shell prompt, type **Mount-Database -Identity 'StudentXX-A\Third Storage Group\Second Mailbox Database'** and press Enter.

25. At the Exchange Management Shell prompt, type **Retry-Queue –Filter { DeliveryType –eq "MAPIDelivery" }** and press Enter.

26. At the Exchange Management Shell prompt, type **Get-Queue** and press Enter.

Question 9	*Which message is no longer in the queue?*

27. At the Exchange Management Shell prompt, type **Get-Message** and press Enter. Note the information regarding the Queue Test 2 message.

28. At the Exchange Management Shell prompt, type **Remove-Message –Identity 'StudentXX-A*queue_number**message_number*'** and press Enter where *queue_number* and *message_number* are the queue and message numbers from the output of the Get-Message cmdlet in the previous step.

29. Close the Exchange Management Shell.

Exercise 11.3	Tracking Messages
Overview	As an Exchange administrator, there will be times when you will need to identify emails that have passed through the email queues on your Hub role servers.
	In this exercise, you will track messages that have been sent and received on your Hub role server by Administrator using the Message Tracking tool in the Microsoft Exchange Troubleshooting Assistant as well as by using cmdlets within the Exchange Management Shell.
	To complete this lab exercise, StudentXX-A must be started and have network access.
Completion time	10 minutes

1. On StudentXX-A, log in as Administrator.

2. Click Start, All Programs, Microsoft Exchange Server 2007, and then click Exchange Management Console.

3. In the console tree pane, highlight Toolbox. In the detail pane, double click Message Tracking under the Mail flow tools section.

4. At the Microsoft Exchange Troubleshooting Assistant window, select the checkbox next to Sender and type **Administrator** in the related dialog box.

5. Click Resolve Sender to fill in the full email address for Administrator.

6. Ensure that RECEIVE is selected in the EventID drop-down box and deselect Start.

7. Click Next.

8. Examine the information about the messages received from Administrator. You may need to select column handles to widen certain columns that you wish to read.

9. When you are finished, click Go Back.

10. Select SEND in the EventID drop-down box and click Next.

11. Examine the information about the messages sent from Administrator. You may need to select column handles to widen certain columns that you wish to read.

12. When you are finished, select a single message and click Next. Notice that you are presented with another message tracking page that searches by MessageID for any messages that have the same MessageID as the message that you selected.

13. Deselect Start and click Next to view messages that have passed through the email queues on your system with the specified MessageID.

14. When finished, close the Microsoft Exchange Troubleshooting Assistant window and close the Exchange Management Console.

15. Click Start, All Programs, Microsoft Exchange Server 2007, and then click Exchange Management Shell.

16. At the Exchange Management Shell prompt, type **Get-MessageTrackingLog –EventId 'RECEIVE' –Sender 'Administrator@StudentXX.com'** and press Enter.

17. Examine the output and note that it is identical to the output shown by the Microsoft Exchange Troubleshooting Assistant in Step 8.

18. At the Exchange Management Shell prompt, type **Get-MessageTrackingLog –EventId 'SEND' –Sender 'Administrator@StudentXX.com'** and press Enter.

19. Examine the output and note that it is identical to the output shown by the Microsoft Exchange Troubleshooting Assistant in Step 11.

20. Close the Exchange Management Shell.

Exercise 11.4	Monitoring Client Connectivity
Overview	Monitoring client connectivity is an important ongoing task for Exchange administrators in performing capacity planning as well as a common procedure in troubleshooting client connectivity.
	In this exercise, you will monitor client connectivity using Outlook, protocol-related cmdlets, and SMTP protocol logs.
	To complete this lab exercise, StudentXX-A and StudentXX-B must be started and have network access.
Completion time	15 minutes

1.   On StudentXX-A, log in as Administrator.

2.   Click Start, All Programs, Microsoft Office, and then click Microsoft Office Outlook 2007.

3.   While holding down the Ctrl key, right click the Outlook icon within the notification area in the lower right corner of the Windows desktop and select Connection Status.

4.   Examine the results and close the Microsoft Exchange Connection Status window.

5.   While holding down the Ctrl key, right click the Outlook icon within the notification area in the lower right corner of the Windows desktop and select Test E-Mail AutoConfiguration.

6.   At the Test E-Mail AutoConfiguration window, click Test and examine the results.

7.   Close the Test E-Mail AutoConfiguration window and close Outlook 2007.

8.   Click Start, All Programs, Microsoft Exchange Server 2007, and then click Exchange Management Shell.

9.   At the Exchange Management Shell prompt, type **Test-MAPIConnectivity** and press Enter. Examine the output.

10.   At the Exchange Management Shell prompt, type **Test-POPConnectivity** and press Enter. Examine the output.

> **NOTE**
>
> *If you receive an error when connecting to your CAS role server using the Test-POPConnectivity cmdlet, you will need to create a new system user account for testing by running the New-TestCASConnectivityUser.ps1 script at the Exchange Management Shell prompt.*

11.   At the Exchange Management Shell prompt, type **Test-IMAPConnectivity** and press Enter. Examine the output.

12.   At the Exchange Management Shell prompt, type **Test-OWAConnectivity** and press Enter. Examine the output.

13. At the Exchange Management Shell prompt, type **Test-WebServicesConnectivity** and press Enter. Examine the output.

14. At the Exchange Management Shell prompt, type **Get-Mailbox 'Tiger Smith' | Test-MAPIConnectivity | Format-List** and press Enter. Examine the output.

15. At the Exchange Management Shell prompt, type **Test-IMAPConnectivity –Client AccessServer 'StudentXX-A' –MailboxCredential:(Get-Credential StudentXX.com\ tiger.smith) | Format-List** and press Enter. Supply the password **Secret123** when prompted. Examine the output.

16. At the Exchange Management Shell prompt, type **Set-ReceiveConnector 'Client StudentXX-A' –ProtocolLoggingLevel 'Verbose'** and press Enter.

17. At the Exchange Management Shell prompt, type **Set-ReceiveConnector 'Default StudentXX-A' –ProtocolLoggingLevel 'Verbose'** and press Enter.

18. Close the Exchange Management Shell.

19. Click Start, All Programs, and then Outlook Express.

20. Click Create Mail to compose a new email. Type **administrator@StudentXX.com** in the To dialog box, type **Test IMAP Message** in the Subject dialog box, and click Send.

21. Click Send/Recv.

22. Close Outlook Express.

23. Click Start and then click My Computer. Navigate to the **C:\Program Files\Microsoft\ Exchange Server\TransportRoles\Logs\ProtocolLog\SmtpReceive** directory.

24. Double click on the log file in the directory and examine its contents. Close Notepad when finished.

Exercise 11.5   Creating Usage Reports

Overview	Monitoring the usage of your Mailbox, Hub, and CAS role servers is important to ensure that you can implement the appropriate usage restrictions or upgrade your Exchange infrastructure before server capacity is exhausted.
	In this exercise, you will generate usage reports on mailbox, top mailbox, email relay, and protocol usage.
	To complete this lab exercise, StudentXX-A and StudentXX-B must be started and have network access. In addition, you must ensure that Microsoft Excel is installed on StudentXX-A.
Completion time	60 minutes

1. On StudentXX-A, log in as Administrator.

2. Click Start, All Programs, Microsoft Exchange Server 2007, and then click Exchange Management Shell.

3. At the Exchange Management Shell prompt, type **Get-MailboxStatistics –Database 'StudentXX-A\First Storage Group\Mailbox Database' | Select-Object DisplayName, ItemCount,TotalItemSize | Export-CSV 'C:\StudentXX-A_Mailbox_Database_ Usage. csv' -NoType** and press Enter.

> **Question 10**
>
> *Briefly explain what the previous command accomplished.*

4. At the Exchange Management Shell prompt, type **Get-MailboxStatistics –Database 'StudentXX-A\Third Storage Group\Second Mailbox Database' | Select-Object DisplayName,ItemCount,TotalItemSize | Export-CSV 'C:\StudentXX-A_Second_ Mailbox_Database_Usage.csv' -NoType** and press Enter.

5. At the Exchange Management Shell prompt, type **Get-MailboxStatistics –Database 'StudentXX-B\First Storage Group\Mailbox Database' | Select-Object DisplayName, ItemCount,TotalItemSize | Export-CSV 'C:\StudentXX-B_Mailbox_Database_ Usage. csv' -NoType** and press Enter.

6. At the Exchange Management Shell prompt, type **Get-MailboxStatistics –Database 'StudentXX-B\Third Storage Group\Second Mailbox Database' | Select-Object DisplayName,ItemCount,TotalItemSize | Export-CSV 'C:\StudentXX-B_Second_ Mailbox_Database_Usage.csv' -NoType** and press Enter.

7. At the Exchange Management Shell prompt, type **Get-ExchangeServer | Get-Mailbox Statistics | Where { $_.TotalItemSize –ge 350MB } | Sort-Object TotalItemSize | Export-CSV 'C:\StudentXX.com_Large_Mailbox_Sizes.csv' -NoType** and press Enter.

> **Question 11**
>
> *Which mailboxes will be included in the C:\StudentXX .com_Large_Mailbox_Sizes.csv file and in what order?*

8. At the Exchange Management Shell prompt, type **Get-ExchangeServer | Get-Mailbox Statistics | Where { $_.ItemCount –ge 1000 } | Sort-Object ItemCount | Export-CSV 'C:\StudentXX.com_Large_Mailbox_Messages.csv' -NoType** and press Enter.

> **Question 12**
>
> *Which mailboxes will be included in the C:\StudentXX .com_Large_Mailbox_Messages.csv file and in what order?*

9. At the Exchange Management Shell prompt, type **Get-MessageTrackingLog –Server 'StudentXX-A' –EventID 'SUBMIT' | Group Sender | Export-CSV 'C:\StudentXX-A_TopSenders.csv' -NoType** and press Enter.

> **Question 13**   *Briefly explain what the previous command accomplished.*

10. At the Exchange Management Shell prompt, type **Get-MessageTrackingLog –Server 'StudentXX-B' –EventID 'SUBMIT' | Group Sender | Export-CSV 'C:\StudentXX-B_TopSenders.csv' -NoType** and press Enter.

11. At the Exchange Management Shell prompt, type **Get-MessageTrackingLog –Server 'StudentXX-A' –EventID 'RECEIVE' | Group Sender | Export-CSV 'C:\StudentXX-A_TopReceivers.csv' -NoType** and press Enter.

> **Question 14**   *Briefly explain what the previous command accomplished.*

12. At the Exchange Management Shell prompt, type **Get-MessageTrackingLog –Server 'StudentXX-B' –EventID 'RECEIVE' | Group Sender | Export-CSV 'C:\Student XX-B_TopReceivers.csv' -NoType** and press Enter.

13. At the Exchange Management Shell prompt, type **Get-CASMailbox | Select-Object Name,ActiveSyncEnabled,OWAEnabled,POPEnabled,IMAPEnabled,MAPIEnabled | Export-CSV 'C:\Mailbox_User_Protocols.csv' - NoType** and press Enter.

> **Question 15**   *Briefly explain what the previous command accomplished.*

14. Close the Exchange Management Shell.

15. Open each of the CSV files that you have created using Microsoft Excel. Next, use the appropriate functions within Microsoft Excel to format the data and columns (fields) for presentation. For simplicity, ensure that each file is contained within a different spreadsheet in your Excel workbook named for the report.

    The first spreadsheet should list the general mailbox usage by storage group using the data in the following files:

    - C:\StudentXX-A_Mailbox_Database_Usage.csv

    - C:\StudentXX-A_Second_Mailbox_Database_Usage.csv

- C:\StudentXX-B_Mailbox_Database_Usage.csv

- C:\StudentXX-B_Second_Mailbox_Database_Usage.csv

The second spreadsheet should list the top 10 mailboxes within your organization by size and number of messages using the data in the following files:

- C:\StudentXX.com_Large_Mailbox_Sizes.csv

- C:\StudentXX.com_Large_Mailbox_Messages.csv

The third spreadsheet should list the senders and receivers by Hub role server using the data in the following files:

- C:\StudentXX-A_TopSenders.csv

- C:\StudentXX-B_TopSenders.csv

- C:\StudentXX-A_TopReceivers.csv

- C:\StudentXX-B_TopReceivers.csv

The fourth spreadsheet should list the client access protocols enabled for mailbox users across the entire organization using the data in the following file:

- C:\Mailbox_User_Protocols.csv

16. Save and print your spreadsheets. When finished, close Microsoft Excel.

LAB REVIEW QUESTIONS

Completion time   15 minutes

1. Describe what you learned by completing this lab.

2. If the number of messages within the email queues on one of your Hub role servers grows continuously, what is the likely cause?

3. Explain why message tracking is likely to be performed using cmdlets rather than using the Message Tracking utility.

4. What would have happened if you tested POP connectivity for the Tiger Smith user in Lab Exercise 11.4?

5. In Lab Exercise 11.5 Steps 7 and 8, why was the CSV file created blank?

LAB CHALLENGE 11.1: CREATING SERVER REPORTS

Completion time	30 minutes

In Lesson 11, you learned a large number of cmdlets within the Exchange Management Shell that can be used to generate information regarding server configuration, health, viruses, and spam. Select four of these cmdlets, execute them on the appropriate Exchange servers (StudentXX-A, StudentXX-B, and StudentXX-C), and redirect their output into a CSV file. Next, import the information in Microsoft Excel and format it for presentation.

LAB 12
CONFIGURING MOBILE ACCESS AND UNIFIED MESSAGING

This lab contains the following exercises and activities:

Exercise 12.1   Configuring ActiveSync

Exercise 12.2   Configuring Unified Messaging

Lab Review Questions

BEFORE YOU BEGIN

Lab 12 assumes that setup has been completed as specified in the setup document and that StudentXX-A, StudentXX-B, and StudentXX-C have connectivity to the classroom network and the Internet. Moreover, Lab 12 assumes that you have completed the exercises in previous labs.

> **NOTE**
>
> *In this lab, you will see the characters XX. When you see these characters, substitute the two-digit number assigned to your computer.*

SCENARIO

In Lab 5, you configured ActiveSync protocol support for several of your mailbox users. In this lab, you will configure ActiveSync support on your CAS role servers as well as restrict the functionality of ActiveSync for those users with the ActiveSync protocol enabled by creating and applying an ActiveSync policy to them.

Additionally, you will configure the Unified Messaging (UM) role on StudentXX-A using nonPBX-specific parameters to experiment with the implementation of UM within Exchange Server 2007.

After completing this lab, you will be able to:

- Configure the ActiveSync protocol on the CAS role servers within your organization

- Configure and apply ActiveSync policies to the mailbox users within your organization

- Configure the UM components within Exchange Server 2007

Estimated lab time: 40 minutes

Exercise 12.1	Configuring ActiveSync
Overview	Several of your users must have access to their mailbox via their smartphone and the ActiveSync protocol. As a result, you must configure the ActiveSync virtual server on StudentXX-A and StudentXX-B to allow for remote connections as well as allow access to file servers within the organization.
	In addition, you wish to ensure that all smartphone devices use passwords that are at least four characters long and that password recovery is possible in the event that a user forgets his or her password. Moreover, you wish to restrict the use of the camera, Internet sharing, and remote desktop features on the smartphones within your organization as well as prevent users from configuring personal email accounts on their smartphones.
	To satisfy these requirements you plan on implementing an ActiveSync policy that has the appropriate restrictions. However, this ActiveSync policy must allow for older smartphones that cannot implement all restrictions. Additionally, Sophia Boren must be exempt from the restrictions within this ActiveSync policy.
	To complete this lab exercise, StudentXX-A and StudentXX-B must be started and have network access.
Completion time	15 minutes

1. On StudentXX-A, log in as Administrator.

2. Click Start, All Programs, Microsoft Exchange Server 2007, and then click Exchange Management Console. The Exchange Management Console window appears.

3. In the console tree pane, expand Server Configuration and highlight Client Access.

4. In the action pane, select StudentXX-A in the detail pane and highlight the Exchange ActiveSync tab in the work pane.

5. Highlight Microsoft-Server-ActiveSync in the work pane and click Properties in the action pane.

6. At the General tab of Microsoft-Server-ActiveSync Properties, ensure that **https:// StudentXX-A.StudentXX.com/Microsoft-Server-ActiveSync** is listed in the Internal URL and External URL dialog boxes to allow for local and remote ActiveSync access.

7. Highlight the Remote File Servers tab and click the Configure button. Type **StudentXX.com** in the Internal Domain Suffix List window, click Add, and click OK.

8. Click OK to close the Microsoft-Server-ActiveSync Properties window.

9. Using the procedure outlined in Steps 4 to 8, configure the same ActiveSync functionality on StudentXX-B (use the URL **https://StudentXX-B.StudentXX.com/Microsoft-Server-ActiveSync**).

10. In the console tree pane, expand Organization Configuration and highlight Client Access.

11. In the action pane, click New Exchange ActiveSync Mailbox Policy.

12. At the New Exchange ActiveSync Mailbox Policy window, type **StudentXX ActiveSync Policy** in the Mailbox policy name dialog box. Next, select the following options:

    - Allow non-provisional devices

    - Require password

    - Enable password recovery

Question 1	What is the default minimum password length?

Question 2	By default, how much idle time will pass before policy users must reenter their password on their smartphone to unlock it?

13. Review your settings and click New.

14. Click Finish to close the New Exchange ActiveSync Mailbox Policy window.

15. Highlight StudentXX ActiveSync Policy in the detail pane and click Set as Default in the action pane.

16. Highlight StudentXX ActiveSync Policy in the detail pane and click Properties in the action pane.

Question 3	Does this policy allow access to Windows file shares and SharePoint services by default?

17. Highlight the Sync Settings tab. Select **Limit message size to (KB)** and type **2048** in the associated dialog box.

18. Highlight the Device tab and deselect **Allow camera, Allow Internet sharing from the device**, and **Allow remote desktop from the device**. Next, select Disable in the Allow Bluetooth drop-down box.

19. Highlight the Advanced tab, deselect **Allow consumer mail**, and click OK.

20. In the console tree pane, expand Recipient Configuration and highlight Mailbox.

21. In the result pane, highlight Sophia Boren and click Properties in the action pane.

22. At the mailbox user properties, highlight the Mailbox Features tab, select Exchange ActiveSync, and click Properties.

Question 4	*What is the default policy assigned to Sophia Boren and why?*

23. Click Browse, select Default, and click OK.

24. Click OK to close the Exchange ActiveSync Properties window.

25. Click OK to close the user properties window.

Question 5	*What restrictions are within the Default ActiveSync policy?*

26. Close the Exchange Management Console.

Exercise 12.2	**Configuring Unified Messaging**
Overview	Although the configuration of UM is largely dependent on the type and configuration of your PBX system, you should practice some of the more common UM configuration tasks within Exchange Server 2007 in a test environment with sample data before performing the necessary research for your own PBX system and configuring UM functionality within your organization.
	As a result, you plan to create a test configuration that demonstrates how UM dial plans, UM IP gateways, UM mailbox policies, UM auto attendants, and mailbox users work together to achieve UM functionality.
	To complete this lab exercise, StudentXX-A and StudentXX-B must be started and have network access.
Completion time	15 minutes

1. On StudentXX-A, log in as Administrator.

2. Click Start, All Programs, Microsoft Exchange Server 2007, and then click Exchange Management Console.

3. In the console tree pane, expand Organization Configuration and highlight Unified Messaging.

4. In the action pane, click New UM Dial Plan.

5. At the New UM Dial Plan window, type **StudentXX UM Dial Plan** in the Name dialog box, type **4** in the Number of digits in extension numbers dialog box and click New.

6. Click Finish to close the New UM Dial Plan window.

7. In the console tree pane, expand Server Configuration and highlight Unified Messaging.

8. In the detail pane, highlight StudentXX-A and click Properties in the action pane.

9. In the properties of StudentXX-A, highlight the UM Settings tab.

10. Click Add, select StudentXX UM Dial Plan, and click OK.

11. Click OK to close the server properties window.

12. In the console tree pane, expand Organization Configuration and highlight Unified Messaging.

13. In the action pane, click New UM IP Gateway.

14. At the New UM IP Gateway window, type **Test UM IP Gateway** in the Name dialog box, select Fully qualified domain name (FQDN) and type **TestUMIPgateway. StudentXX.com** in the associated dialog box.

Question 6	What does TestUMIPgateway.StudentXX.com represent?

15. Click Browse, select StudentXX UM Dial Plan, and click OK.

16. Review your settings and click New.

17. Click Finish to close the New UM IP Gateway window.

18. In the action pane, click New UM Mailbox Policy.

19. At the New UM Mailbox Policy window, type **Test UM Mailbox Policy** in the Name dialog box.

20. Click Browse, select StudentXX UM Dial Plan, and click OK.

21. Click New.

22. Click Finish to close the New UM Mailbox Policy window.

23. In the action pane, click New UM Auto Attendant.

24. At the New UM Auto Attendant window, type **Test UM Auto Attendant** in the Name dialog box.

25. Click Browse, select StudentXX UM Dial Plan, and click OK.

26. In the Extension numbers dialog box, type **1234** and click Add.

Question 7	What will happen when users access the extension 1234?

27. Select **Create auto attendant as enabled** and **Create auto attendant as speech enabled** and click New.

28. Click Finish to close the New UM Auto Attendant window.

29. In the console tree pane, expand Recipient Configuration, Mailbox, and highlight Tiger Smith in the detail pane.

30. In the action pane, click Enable Unified Messaging.

31. At the Enable Unified Messaging window, click Browse, select Test UM Mailbox Policy, and click OK.

32. Click **Manually specify PIN**, type **4491** in the dialog box, and click Next. Note that the default PIN length could vary between versions of Exchange.

Question 8	When must Tiger Smith enter the PIN 4491?

33. At the Extension Configuration page, type **2301** in the dialog box to indicate that extension 2301 is attached to Tiger Smith's mailbox and click Next.

34. At the Enable Unified Messaging page, review your settings and click Enable.

35. Click Finish to close the Enable Unified Messaging window.

36. Close the Exchange Management Console.

LAB REVIEW QUESTIONS

Completion time   10 minutes

1. Describe what you learned by completing this lab.

2. What must you have in order to benefit from the configuration options on the Device and Advanced tabs in Lab Exercise 12.1?

3. In Lab Exercise 12.2, what could you do to make your UM role fault tolerant?

LAB 13
CONFIGURING HIGH AVAILABILITY

This lab contains the following exercises and activities:

Exercise 13.1   Configuring Local Continuous Replication

Exercise 13.2   Configuring Standby Continuous Replication

Lab Review Questions

BEFORE YOU BEGIN

Lab 13 assumes that setup has been completed as specified in the setup document and that StudentXX-A, StudentXX-B, and StudentXX-C have connectivity to the classroom network and the Internet. Moreover, Lab 13 assumes that you have completed the exercises in previous labs.

> **NOTE**
>
> *In this lab, you will see the characters XX. When you see these characters, substitute the two-digit number assigned to your computer.*

SCENARIO

Although backups provide protection for mailbox and public folder information, they are often time consuming to restore after a failure. As a result, you can configure high-availability technologies to provide continuous access to data in the event that a server role or database fails.

In this lab, you will configure two different high-availability technologies: Local Continuous Replication (LCR) and Standby Continuous Replication (SCR) using the StudentXX-A and StudentXX-B Mailbox role servers in your organization.

After completing this lab, you will be able to:

- Configure Local Continuous Replication on a Mailbox role server

- Configure Standby Continuous Replication on a Mailbox role server

Estimated lab time: 40 minutes

Exercise 13.1	Configuring Local Continuous Replication
Overview	Local Continuous Replication (LCR) can be easily configured on a Mailbox role server to provide continuous data backup to a second database.
	In this exercise, you will configure LCR for the Second Mailbox Database within the Third Storage Group on StudentXX-A, reseed the LCR database copy, and view the related files on the hard drive. Next, to simulate an LCR restore operation, you will switch the original database and LCR database paths so that users can immediately access their emails from the LCR database copy.
	To complete this lab exercise, StudentXX-A must be started and have network access.
Completion time	15 minutes

1. On StudentXX-A, log in as Administrator.

2. Click Start, All Programs, Microsoft Exchange Server 2007, and then click Exchange Management Console. The Exchange Management Console window appears.

3. In the console tree pane, expand Server Configuration and highlight Mailbox.

4. In the detail pane, highlight StudentXX-A and select Third Storage Group in the work pane.

5. In the action pane, click Enable Local Continuous Replication.

6. When the Enable Storage Group Local Continuous Replication window appears, click Next.

7. At the Set Paths page, click Browse next to the Local Continuous Replication system files path dialog box, navigate to C:\, click Make New Folder, and type **LCR**. Select the LCR directory and click OK.

8. Click Browse next to the Local Continuous Replication log files path dialog box, navigate to the C:\LCR directory and click OK.

9. Click Next.

10. Ensure that Second Mailbox Database is selected in the Database name dialog box, click Browse next to the Local Continuous Replication log files path dialog box, navigate to the C:\LCR directory, and click OK.

11. At the Enable page, review your selections and click Enable.

12. On the Completion page, click Finish to close the Enable Storage Group Local Continuous Replication window.

13. In the detail pane, highlight StudentXX-A, select Third Storage Group in the work pane, and click Update Storage Group Copy in the action pane.

14. At the Update Storage Group Copy window, select **Delete any existing log files in the target path** and click Next.

15. At the Update Storage Group Copy page, review your selections and click Update. When prompted to overwrite the target database and transaction logs, click Yes.

16. On the Completion page, click Finish to close the Update Storage Group Copy window.

17. Close the Exchange Management Console.

18. Click Start, All Programs, Microsoft Office, and then click Microsoft Office Outlook 2007.

19. In the left pane of Outlook 2007, expand Mailbox—Administrator and highlight Inbox.

20. Click New to compose a new email. Click the To button, select Meg Roombas and click OK. The mailbox for Meg Roombas is within the Second Mailbox Database in the Third Storage Group on StudentXX-A.

21. Type **LCR Test 1** in the Subject dialog box and click Send.

22. Close Outlook 2007.

23. Click Start and click My Computer. Navigate to the C:\LCR directory and ensure that the view option is set to Details in order to see the modification date of each file.

Question 1	*Are there any log files that have been recently shipped to the C:\LCR directory?*

24. Close the My Computer window.

25. Click Start, All Programs, Microsoft Exchange Server 2007, and then click Exchange Management Console. The Exchange Management Console window appears.

26. In the console tree pane, expand Server Configuration and highlight Mailbox.

27. In the detail pane, highlight StudentXX-A, expand Third Storage Group in the work pane, and select the Second Mailbox Database.

28. In the action pane, click Dismount Database and click Yes when prompted.

29. In the work pane, highlight Third Storage Group and click Restore Storage Group Copy from the action pane.

30. At the Restore Storage Group Copy window, select Replace production database path locations with this copy and click Next.

31. At the Restore Storage Group Copy page, review your selections and click Restore.

32. On the Completion page, click Finish to close the Restore Storage Group Copy window.

33. In the detail pane, select Second Mailbox Database under the Third Storage Group and click Mount Database from the action pane.

Question 2	*What path is listed next to the Second Mailbox Database?*

34. Close the Exchange Management Console.

Exercise 13.2   Configuring Standby Continuous Replication

Overview	Standby Continuous Replication (SCR) is similar to LCR in that it uses log shipping to copy data to a redundant storage group and database. However, the redundant storage group and database resides on another Mailbox role server.
	In this lab exercise, you will configure a new storage group and mailbox database on StudentXX-A and configure an SCR copy on StudentXX-B. After testing your SCR copy, you will disable it.
	To complete this lab exercise, StudentXX-A and StudentXX-B must be started and have network access.
Completion time	15 minutes

1. On StudentXX-B, log in as Administrator.

2. Create a directory called C:\SG4.

3. Switch to StudentXX-A and log in as Administrator.

4. Create a directory called C:\SG4.

5. Click Start, All Programs, Microsoft Exchange Server 2007, and then click Exchange Management Shell.

6. At the Exchange Management Shell prompt, type **New-StorageGroup –Server 'Student XX-A' –Name 'Fourth Storage Group' –LogFolderPath 'C:\SG4' –SystemFolderPath 'C:\SG4'** and press Enter.

7. At the Exchange Management Shell prompt, type **New-MailboxDatabase –StorageGroup 'StudentXX-A\Fourth Storage Group' –Name 'Third Mailbox Database' –EdbFilePath 'C:\SG4\Third Mailbox Database.edb'** and press Enter.

8. At the Exchange Management Shell prompt, type **Mount-Database –Identity 'Student XX-A\Third Mailbox Database'** and press Enter.

9. At the Exchange Management Shell prompt, type **Enable-StorageGroupCopy -Identity 'StudentXX-A\Fourth Storage Group' -StandbyMachine 'StudentXX-B' -Replay LagTime 0.0:5:0 -TruncationLagTime 0.8:5:0** and press Enter.

> **Question 3** | *After logs have been shipped from StudentXX-A to StudentXX-B, how long will StudentXX-B wait until replaying them?*

> **Question 4** | *After logs have been replayed by StudentXX-B, how long will StudentXX-B wait until truncating them?*

10. At the Exchange Management Shell prompt, type **New-Mailbox -UserPrincipalName 'test.user@StudentXX.com' -Alias 'test.user' -Database 'StudentXX-A\Fourth Storage Group\Third Mailbox Database' -Name 'Test User' -OrganizationalUnit 'StudentXX. com/Accounting' -FirstName 'Test' -LastName 'User' -DisplayName 'Test User' –Reset PasswordOnNextLogon $true** and press Enter. When prompted for an initial password, type **Secret123** and press Enter.

11. Switch to your session on StudentXX-B and view the contents of the C:\SG4 directory.

> **Question 5** | *What files are present in the C:\SG4 directory on StudentXX-B?*

12. Switch back to your session on StudentXX-A and make the Exchange Management Shell active.

13. At the Exchange Management Shell prompt, type **Disable-StorageGroupCopy -Identity 'StudentXX-A\Fourth Storage Group' -StandbyMachine 'StudentXX-B'** and press Enter.

14. Close the Exchange Management Shell.

LAB REVIEW QUESTIONS

Completion time   10 minutes

1.   Describe what you learned by completing this lab.

2.   What is wrong with using a path of C:\LCR for the LCR storage group and database in Lab Exercise 13.1?

3.   Why did you configure SCR within the Exchange Management Shell in Lab Exercise 13.2?

Notes

Notes

Notes